Functionalism

JONATHAN H. TURNER

Department of Sociology
University of California
at Riverside

ALEXANDRA MARYANSKI

Department of Anthropology
University of California
at Riverside

The Benjamin/Cummings Publishing Company
Menlo Park, California • Reading, Massachusetts
London • Amsterdam • Don Mills, Ontario • Sydney

Editorial/production services by
Phoenix Publishing Services, San Francisco.

Library of Congress Cataloging in Publication Data

Turner, Jonathan H
    Functionalism.

    (The Benjamin/Cummings series in contemporary
sociology)
    1. Functionalism (Social sciences). I. Maryanski,
Alexandra, joint author. II. Title. III. Series.
GN363.T87   301'.01   79-10088
ISBN 0-8053-9338-2

    BCDEFGHIJ–AL–782109

The Benjamin/Cummings Publishing Company
2727 Sand Hill Road
Menlo Park, California 94025

Functionalism

1 · 2010

The Benjamin/Cummings
SERIES IN CONTEMPORARY SOCIOLOGY

General editor: James F. Short, Jr.

To Martha and Paul Zavaski

Contents

Preface

The sociologist, Robert Nisbet, was once moved to comment that "functionalism is, without any doubt, the single most significant body of theory in the social sciences in the present century." This may be an exaggeration, but Nisbet is correct in his implication that much intellectual activity in sociology and anthropology has been carried out under the intellectual banner of functionalism. Indeed, some of the intellectual giants of this and the last century—Comte, Spencer, Durkheim, Malinowski, Radcliffe-Brown, Merton, and Parsons, to name but a few—have engaged in the functional analysis of the social world.

What, then, is functionalism? The actual complexity of this question will become increasingly evident in the following chapters. But ignoring for the moment this complexity, we can offer the following definition: functional analysis examines social phenomena in terms of their consequences for the broader society. What does a kinship system do for society? What does a religious ritual do for society? What are the "functions" of government, of poverty, of classes, or of any social phenomenon?

These questions are not unlike those we ask about biological phenomena. What does the heart do for the body? What is the function of the lymph system? Indeed, as we will soon come to appreciate, functionalism in the social sciences borrowed such questions directly from biology and then asked them of social events in society. In many ways functionalism emerged as the science of the "body social," for it was felt that if insight into the parts of the human body could be achieved by determining how they affected bodily states, the same would be possible for society. By asking the functions of a social structure for the social whole, greater insight into the operation of societies was believed possible.

Such was the promise of functionalism. It offered so much; and yet, as we will come to see, functionalism promised more than it could deliver. Functional analysis often confused rather than classified; and in time, scholars became increasingly disenchanted with functionalism's promise. Today it is not unusual to find commentators arguing that functional analysis has nothing to offer the social sciences. This sentiment is so pervasive that few contemporary social scientists would be willing to proclaim themselves "functionalists." They seemingly have died as an intellectual breed, or retreated into academic closets.

This book is about the emergence, ascendance, and apparent fall of functionalism. Why did it emerge? Why did it prosper and dominate sociology and anthropology? Why did it become the subject of intense criticism? Answers to these questions will provide not only an intellectual portrait of functionalism but also a glimpse into the historical development of sociology and anthropology.

J. H. Turner
A. Maryanski

The Emergence
of Functionalism

Ideas are often responses to social conditions. The brooding and isolated scholar in "the ivory tower" is a myth, created to disguise the degree to which intellectual pursuits are tied to events in the larger social world. Nowhere is the connection between intellectual ideas and social conditions clearer than in the emergence of sociology in general and functional theorizing in particular.

We should not, of course, become carried away with this insight. Ideas do not reflect perfectly broader forces; scholars do create intellectual schemes on their own. And frequently ideas shape the course of human affairs. Yet, if we return to the origins of sociology in the 19th century, we can see the play of economic and political conditions on the emergence of sociology and, in turn, on the development of functionalism.

For indeed, sociology was born in the aftermath of the French Revolution of 1789 and in response to the changes associated with the only slightly less tumultuous Industrial Revolution. Europe was experiencing a dramatic alteration of the social order. The large feudal estates were being eroded. Workers were leaving the countryside for industrial jobs in urban centers. New forms of less aristocratic government were replacing the old nobility. Trade with, and conquest of, the nations of the world was accelerating. It was a time, then, of change, growth, and frequent conflict. Soci-

1

ology did not emerge as a radical doctrine supporting change or encouraging revolution. On the contrary, sociology developed as a reaction to the social turmoil and chaos of the times.[1] We should not be surprised, therefore, that the "science of society" was born as a reaction to the turmoil of the most unstable European society, France.

The French Intellectual Tradition

The French Revolution, coupled with the changes wrought with industrialization and urbanization, had left France in a state of instability. Alarmed by the perpetual turmoil of the late 18th and early 19th centuries, social philosophers began to search for the foundations of social order. They wanted to restore stability and harmony. And in so doing they forged a "collectivist philosophy" that pervades French social thought to this day. While different thinkers advanced varying schemes, the essence of the collectivist philosophy was its concern with morals, ethics, and religion. In order for society to become harmonious, it was asserted, consensus over morals needed to be achieved. People must be guided by a commitment to the same ideas; moreover, they must be willing to subjugate their individual interests to the collective good.

AUGUSTE COMTE AND THE SCIENCE OF SOCIETY

The titular founder of sociology, Auguste Comte, was born into this social and intellectual milieu. Drawing from the renowned socialist, Saint-Simon, Comte strongly supported the conservative philosophy.[2] He was concerned with restoring social equilibrium in France, but he argued that

[1]Perhaps the most eloquent statement of the conservative origins of sociology can be found in Robert Nisbet's work. *See* for example, his *The Sociological Tradition* (New York: Basic Books, 1966).

[2]Most scholars agree that the groundplan for the positive philosophy came from Saint–Simon, Comte's mentor. Comte's brilliance lay not in his ability for the creation of original ideas, but rather in his remarkable ability to synthesize seemingly disparate ones. However, the organismic analogy as a model for the whole of human society was Comte's own creation. For excellent and highly readable accounts of Auguste Comte and his philosophy see Lewis Coser's *Masters of Sociological Thought* (New York: Harcourt, Brace, Jovanovich, 1977); and Howard Becker's and Larry Barnes's, *Social Thought from Lore to Science,* vol. 2 (New York: Dover, 1961).

limited and patchwork social reforms would not be successful. Rather, a complete reorganization of society was necessary.

Such reorganization, however, could only occur with increased understanding of society. We should remember that Comte was not a radical revolutionary, but a conservative who wished to develop a stable basis for the organization of society.[3] Comte thus set out to develop what he termed his "positive philosophy," contained in his six-volume *Course of Positive Philosophy* (1830–1842).[4] In this work, sociology was formally named, and particularly critical for our purposes, the basis for functional theorizing was established.

The emergence of sociology as a science and functionalism as a dominant theoretical perspective were thus intimately tied together. We must, therefore, explore how Comte's creation of the positive philosophy contained the seeds of functional theorizing. To do this we will first examine Comte's doctrine of "social progress" and then his "theory of organicism."

Social Progress and Positivism   Comte's philosophical system, and his plan for societal reorganization, rested upon his vision of social evolution. In his "law of the three stages," Comte asserted that human knowledge about, and explanations of, social phenomena pass through three successive stages: the "theological," "metaphysical," and "positive." In the theological stage, religious or supernatural explanations of the human condition dominate; in the metaphysical stage rational reason and deduction are as-

[3]"Institutions," Comte says, "depend on morals, and morals, in their turn, depend on beliefs. Every scheme of new institutions will therefore be useless so long as morals have not been 'reorganised,' and so long as, to reach this end, a general system of opinions has not been founded, which are accepted by all minds as true ... " Quoted in Levy-Bruhl's, *The Philosophy of Auguste Comte* (Clifton: Augustus Kelley, 1903), p. 4.

[4]The English translation of this monumental work can be found in three volumes by Harriet Martineau under the title, *The Positive Philosophy of Auguste Comte* (London: George Bell and Sons: 1896—originally published in 1853). The main outlines, however, for much of Comte's *Positive Philosophy* were sketched in one of his very early essays, appropriately entitled, "Plan of the Scientific Operations Necessary for Reorganizing Society" (1822). This essay and other important excerpts of his work can be found in Gertrud Lenzer's *Auguste Comte and Positivism: The Essential Writings* (New York: Harper and Row, 1975).

cendant; and in the positive or scientific phase, empirically based knowledge is used to explain social phenomena.[5]

Comte argued that the beginnings of the final stage, the positive, could be seen. Knowledge of the social world must be based upon empirical observations, experimentation, and comparison. Only by attention to actual events in the world would the laws of social organization be discovered.

With the arrival of the positive stage, Comte stated, it was now possible for the first time to have a true "science of society." Unlike the speculative social philosophy of previous times, a social science similar to that of the natural sciences could be developed. And with a true science that could uncover the laws of human organization, deliberate and planned social reorganization could occur. This new science of society that would transform the world and restore stability was termed by Comte, "sociology." Sociology was to uncover the natural laws of social phenomena:[6] "The principle of Sociology consists in conceiving social phenomena as inevitably subjected to natural laws. We must first fix the peculiar character of these laws. To obtain this result, we must extend a truly scientific distinction to social phenomena. . . . " Comte thus welded sociology to empirical inquiry that could generate the laws of human social organization. In turn, these laws could be used to reorganize society and maintain its equilibrium.

We should make several observations about Comte's arguments in order to see how they were to shape the subsequent development of functional analysis. First, most functional writings hold some view of the "good" society or of what the "normal" state of society is. This is inherent in the notion of asking what a social phenomenon "does for"

[5] As Comte notes: "In order to understand the true value and character of the Positive Philosophy, we must take a brief general view of the progressive course of the human mind, regarded as a whole; for no conception can be understood otherwise than through its history. From the study of human intelligence, in all directions, and through all times, the discovery arises of a great fundamental law . . . the law is this:—that each of our leading conceptions,—each branch of our knowledge pass (sic) successively through three different theoretical conditions: the theological, or fictitious; the Metaphysical, or abstract; and the Scientific, or Positive . . . the first is the necessary point of departure of the human understanding; and the third is its fixed and definitive state. The second is merely a state of transition." *The Positive Philosophy of Auguste Comte,* op. cit., p. 2.

[6] Auguste Comte in G. H. Leives's, *Comte's Philosophy of the Sciences* (London: George Bell, 1897), p. 251.

or "contributes to" the social whole. Comte was instrumental in linking sociological analysis to moral purposes: We must use our understanding of social laws to assess the contribution of social structures for the social whole—eliminating those that are "harmful" and creating those that are "good." Second, functional analysis begins with a notion of social equilibrum—whether this be conceptualized as "social integration," "social cohesion," or some other state of stasis. Comte's emphasis on using science to create order, stability, and harmony was certainly important in directing functional analysis to a concern with social integration and equilibrium. These two themes often remain implicit in later functionalisms, but we should remain alert to their influence when we examine in later chapters more elaborate functional schemes.

The 'Theory' of Organicism[7]   A nascent discipline is vulnerable. It has few adherents; it is usually not connected to the intellectual establishment; it threatens scholars in traditional intellectual domains; and it is subject to the unkind criticism of being a new name for the study of phenomena of another discipline. Comte was very sensitive to these problems. In fact, much of his career was devoted to demonstrating that sociology was unique and important, that it was not a new name for the old social philosophizing, and that it was a legitimate science.

Comte employed several strategies to decrease the vulnerability of sociology. One was his insistence that the study of social phenomena could be scientific—thus removing sociology from the more speculative moral philosophy of his time. More important was his effort to show the similarity of sociology to the more respected and established sciences, most particularly to biology. In this vein, Comte postulated a "hierarchy of sciences" in which the sciences could be rank ordered in terms of their emergence and the complexity of the phenomena that they study. Not

[7]The word "organic" first came into the English language as "organical," a synonym for mechanical in the 16th century. By the 18th century, though, mechanical became associated with artificial, while organic took on a physical or biological connotation. The word itself then began to take on more specific connotations with the separation of organ, giving rise to the synonyms organic and organizations. By the 19th century, however, these words became opposed as "natural" versus "planned."

coincidentally, Comte's sociology was to be the "queen science" at the top of the hierarchy, with biology a notch below.[8]

The placement of biology just below sociology was critical for two reasons. First, biology was highly respected. The codification of the Linnean classification system, the systematic cataloging of wide varieties of species, the new discoveries in medicine, and most important, the intellectual debate and excitement preceding Darwin's and Wallace's theory of evolution all made biology the most visible science of the 19th century. We can thus see that it was a shrewd tactic to conceptualize sociology as a direct outgrowth of biology and as even more important in the explanation of the social world. Indeed, sociology would someday guide and direct biology. As he noted:[9] "Biology has hitherto been the guide and preparation for Sociology; but ... Sociology will in the future be rather the type for the ultimate systematisation of Biology."

A second reason for viewing Comte's linking of sociology and biology as important concerns what is termed "the organic analogy."[10] For Comte, society was a type of organism, a "social organism." Biology studies "individual organisms," while sociology examines the "social organism." Comte divided sociology into two distinct parts: "statics" or morphology and "dynamics" or change and progress. This distinction within sociology proper also corresponded to a similar portion in the physics of Comte's time. And in fact, Comte sometimes termed sociology "social physics," thus allying sociology to another respected science. But far more important in Comte's scheme, and in the development of

[8]In Comte's hierarchy, the sciences form a linear progressive series. At the bottom is mathematics followed by astronomy, physics, chemistry, and biology. With the development of sociology, at the top of the hierarchy, the series was complete for sociology was to be "the most logical of all the sciences." *The Positive Philosophy of Auguste Comte,* op. cit., pp. 379 ff.

[9]Auguste Comte, *System of Positive Polity.* Second vol. (New York: Burt Franklin: 1875, original 1852).

[10]It is worth mentioning that the organismic analogy, that of showing a likeness between a living organism and some part of the body social, was not new to the 19th century. Indeed it was used very early in Greek and Hindu writings on social thought, in early Christian writings, and frequently during the Middle Ages. Again in the 18th century, organic imagery was clearly evident in the writings of Hobbes and Rousseau who conceptualized a resemblance between the political state and the animated living organism. Comte was first, however, to conceptualize the whole of society as analogous to a giant living organism.

functionalism, was his attempt to demonstrate how society is a kind of organism. As he argued:[11]

> We have thus established a true correspondence between the Statical Analysis of the Social Organism in Sociology, and that of the Individual Organism in Biology ... If we take the best ascertained points in Biology, we may decompose structure anatomically into *elements, tissues,* and *organs.* We have the same things in the Social Organism; and may even use the same names.

Comte then would seek the structural analogue of biological elements, such as elements, tissues, and organs, in the "social organism." For Comte the family was the basic social element, social power and stratification were the tissues, and the cities were the organs. As Comte emphasized:[12] "I shall treat the Social Organism as definitely composed of the Families which are the true elements or cells, next of the Classes or Castes which are its proper tissues, and lastly of the Cities and Communes which are its real organs."

This vision of the social organism was a decisive moment in sociological theorizing. It connoted a view of the social world as a complex social whole with each part contributing to its maintenance or survival. When society is seen as an organism, it is a short analytical step to asking: What does this or that structure "do for" or "contribute to" the society. Such questions are at the heart of functional theorizing; and while Comte did not draw out the full implications of his organismic thinking, subsequent scholars were to transform Comte's initial comparisons into functionalism, sociology's first theoretical perspective.

To appreciate just how Comte's ideas were transformed, we must shift for the moment from the European continent of the 1830s and 1840s to England. We will return again to France in the last decade of the 19th century and examine the work of Émile Durkheim, but first we must explore the middle years of the 19th century and work of Herbert Spencer, the crucial link between Auguste Comte and Émile Durkheim.

[11]Comte, *System of Positive Polity,* op. cit., pp. 239–240.
[12]Ibid., p. 242.

The British Tradition

Unlike France, English society had not experienced a massive revolution. Although the Industrial Revolution profoundly reorganized Britain, as it had France, considerably less disruption to the fabric of the society had occurred. Indeed, by the 1860s industrialism had ushered in a period of comparative prosperity and affluence. And by the mid-Victorian era, Britain had settled comfortably into a complacent mood.[13]

We should not underestimate the significance of this mood. The apparent success of industrial capitalism seemed to vindicate the faith of 18th-century thinkers in progress. Prosperity also legitimated the economic and philosophical doctrine of utilitarianism which, in broad strokes, argued for the unregulated competition among individuals in the marketplace. Moreover, progress and prosperity were to fit rather nicely with the theory of biological evolution as it was being developed independently by Darwin and Wallace. Thus, by the middle of the last century several forces were simultaneously influencing intellectual discourse in England: prosperity affirmed notions of 18th-century faith in progress; utilitarian doctrines had been "confirmed"; and the theory of biological evolution was emerging. In turn, these themes were to shape the work of Herbert Spencer, the first significant English sociologist and the first social scientist to introduce the concept of "function" into the social sciences.

HERBERT SPENCER AND STRUCTURAL–FUNCTIONALISM

Herbert Spencer was, to a degree that he would not admit, in Comte's debt.[14] Somewhat begrudgingly, he gave Comte

---

[13]See Coser, op. cit., p. 112, for a discussion of the intellectual mood in England during the Victorian era.

[14]Spencer rejected all suggestions that Comte had heavily influenced him. In his article, "Reasons for Dissenting from the Philosophy of M. Comte" published in 1864, Spencer admits that although he disagrees with Comte "in all those fundamental views that are peculiar to him," he agrees with him "in sundry minor views" after which he lists the areas in which he concurs with Comte's philosophy. Further, he notes that despite his criticism of Comte's work: "Let it by no means be supposed from all I have said, that I do not regard M. Comte's speculations as of great value. True or untrue, his system as a whole, has doubtless produced important and salutary revolutions of thought in many minds; and will doubtless do so in many more" (Spencer: 24). We suspect, however, that Herbert Spencer protested a bit too much about how little of an influence Comte was on

credit for the word Sociology, for the conception of a social consensus, and for the idea of a social science modeled after the traditional sciences. Spencer also retained Comte's concern with empirical data as the basis on which the science of society should be developed.

Yet, Spencer was the leading spokesman for laissez-faire capitalism and a powerful advocate of utilitarianism. He firmly believed, as he once said, in the "survival of the fittest," maintaining that competition among free, self-seeking individuals would lead to the most efficient society.[15] But this libertarian philosophy posed, as we shall shortly see, a contradiction to his organicism. Organismic thinking emphasizes that the social whole operates through the functional integration and cooperation of its parts, whereas utilitarianism emphasizes competition among self-seeking actors who perpetually pursue their own self-interest while ignoring the collective interests of the whole. Spencer was never able to resolve this fundamental contradiction in his sociology, but he was to extend the organismic analogy explicitly toward a form of functional analysis.

Spencer's Organic Analogizing Spencer developed several organic analogies, most of which paralleled Comte's distinction between social statics and dynamics. With respect to social statics or morphology, Spencer developed a

---

him. For example, when discussing the work of Comte he notes: "There are, I believe, in the part of his writings which I have read, various incidental thoughts of great depth and value; and I doubt not that were I to read more of his writings, I should find many others" (ibid.). Spencer then followed the above quote with a detailed footnote listing in detail exactly what he had read of Comte's work.

[15]While many would disagree, it should be mentioned that Spencer came very close to formulating the theory of evolution before Darwin. In Spencer's *An Autobiography* (1904), he reflects upon the publication of the *Origin of Species* by commenting at one point on how very close he came to the principle of natural selection: " ... the *Origin of Species* was published. That reading it gave me great satisfaction may be safely inferred. Whether there was any set-off to this great satisfaction, I cannot now say; for I have quite forgotten the ideas and feelings I had. Up to that time, or rather up to the time at which the papers by Mr. Darwin and Mr. Wallace, read before the Linnean Society, had become known to me, I held that the sole cause of organic evolution is the inheritance of functionally-produced modifications. The *Origin of Species* made it clear to me that I was wrong ... whether proof that what I had supposed to be the sole cause, could be at best but a part cause, gave me any annoyance, I cannot remember; nor can I remember whether I was vexed by the thought that in 1852 I had failed to carry further the idea then expressed, *that among human beings the survival of those who are the select of their generation is a cause of development.*" (50, our emphasis.)

list of similarities between the social and individual "organisms." This list is paraphrased below:[16]

1. Both society and individual organisms can be distinguished from inorganic matter, for both grow and develop.
2. In both society and organisms an increase in size means an increase in complexity and differentiation.
3. In both, a progressive differentiation in structure is accompanied by a differentiation in function.
4. In both, parts of the whole are interdependent with a change in one part affecting other parts.
5. In both, each part of the whole is also a microsociety or organism in and of itself.
6. And in both organisms and societies, the life of the whole can be destroyed but the parts will live on for a while.

Not only did Spencer emphasize these broad points of comparison, but he also tended to engage in rather detailed comparisons between biological and social structures. For example, he once compared the financial system of industrial England to the vaso-motor nerves of the human body. As he wrote:[17]

The general law as discovered by Ludwig and Loven, is that when by the nerves of sensation there is sent inwards that impression which accompanies the activity of a part, there is reflected back to the part, along its vaso-motor nerves, an influence by which its minute arteries are suddenly dilated; and at the same time, through the vaso-motor nerves going to all inactive parts, there is sent an influence which slightly constricts the arteries supplying them: thus diminishing the flow of blood where it is not wanted, that the flow may be increased where it is wanted. In the social organism, or rather in such a developed organism as our own in modern times, this kind of regulation is effected by the system of banks and associated financial bodies which lend out capital. When a local industry, called into unusual activity by increased consumption of its products, makes demands first of

[16]Jonathan H. Turner, *The Structure of Sociological Theory* (Homewood, Ill.: Dorsey Press, 1974), pp. 16–17.

[17]Herbert Spencer, "The Regulating System" in *The Works of H. Spencer,* vol. 6 (Osnabrück: Otto Zeller, 1966), p. 534.

all on local banks, these, in response to the impressions caused by the rising activity conspicuous around them open more freely those channels. . . .

This kind of detailed analogizing was to be carried to its logical extreme, and to its intellectual death, by followers of Spencer, such as Worms, Lilienfield, and Schaffle.[18] But far more important than the specifics of Spencer's analogizing is what he did with his organismic analogy. In his general comparisons between the individual and social organisms, Spencer began to distinguish between "structure" and "function." It is in this distinction that the essence of functionalism resides: Structures have functions for maintaining the social whole. Spencer must be credited with this distinction, for he stressed that changes in structure involve changes in the function of that structure for the social whole:[19]

Changes of structure cannot occur without changes of functions. . . . If organization consists in such a construction of the whole that its parts can carry on mutually-dependent actions, then in proportion as organization is high there must go a dependence of each part upon the rest so great that separation is fatal; and conversely. This truth is equally well shown in the individual organism and in the social organism.

Thus, structure and function are distinguished in Spencer's work, a separation which was later to become more thoroughly developed by Émile Durkheim, but which provided the basis for functionalism as a distinctive orientation in the social sciences. In addition to this critical distinction, Spencer introduced another concept from biological terminology into sociology: the concept of functional "needs":[20] "There can be no true conception of a structure without a true conception of its function. To understand how an organization originated and developed, it is requi-

---

[18]*See* Barnes and Becker, op. cit., p. 679; and Francis Coker, *Organismic Theories of the State* (New York: AMS Press, 1967). It should perhaps be noted, however, that early in his career Durkheim, who was to reject Spencer's utilitarianism, was to embrace Schaffle's organicism which had been borrowed from Spencer.

[19]Herbert Spencer, "Social Function" in *The Works of H. Spencer,* vol. 6 (Osnabrück: Otto Zeller, 1966, original 1876), p. 473.

[20]Herbert Spencer, op. cit., vol. 8, pp. 1–2.

site to understand the *need* subserved at the outset and afterwards" (emphasis added).

Analysis of social phenomena must therefore recognize that "needs" of the social organism are critical in determining why a structure should exist and persist. This concept was to become one of the most controversial of the functional orientation, since it easily could be taken to imply that events are caused by the needs they meet. We shall frequently have occasion to return to this issue.

We should also mention a second line of organismic analogizing conducted by Spencer. Spencer came very close to discovering the theory of evolution before Darwin; and indeed, Darwin explicitly discusses Spencer's work in *On the Origin of Species.* Spencer saw that competition among individuals led to their social differentiation—the "fittest" assuming social prominence and the less "fit" occupying menial positions. After the publication of Darwin's *On the Origin of Species,* this line of thinking was later to become "social Darwinism," although its basic precepts were formulated prior to Darwin's great breakthrough. It is in such references to conflict among individuals leading to the "survival of the fittest"—Spencer's, not Darwin's phrase—that Spencer's utilitarian and libertarian philosophy became most evident.

A third line of organismic analogizing paralleled Comte's discussion of social dynamics. For Spencer, societies evolve as living organisms, from simple to complex forms: "Societies, like living bodies, begin as germs originate from masses which are extremely minute ... that out of small wandering hordes have arisen the largest societies."[21] Indeed almost all of Spencer's detailed analysis of primitive societies was designed to show the operation of his grand "law" of social evolution which involved a "change from a state of relatively indefinite, incoherent, homogeneity to a state of relatively definite, coherent, heterogeneity."

While Spencer did not explicitly develop the connections

---

[21]Herbert Spencer, op. cit., p. 451. Spencer, foreshadowing Durkheim, recognized that in preliterate societies each part is an independent unit while in industrial societies there is a dependence of parts: "In low aggregates, both individual and social, the actions of the parts are but little dependent on one another; whereas in developed aggregates of both kinds, that combination of actions which constitutes the life of the whole, makes possible the component actions which constitute the lives of the parts" (ibid., 475).

between increased competition and the emergence of the division of labor—or "the definite coherent, heterogeneity" of his law—subsequent theorists, such as Durkheim, were to expand upon Spencer's provocative ideas. Durkheim, in particular, was to pull each separate strand from Spencer's analysis and weave them into an expanded version of functional analysis. The key elements that Spencer brought to functionalism from his organismic analogizing can be summarized as follows:

1. Society is a *system.* It is a coherent whole of connected parts.
2. This system can only be understood in terms of the operation of specific structures, each of which has a function for maintaining the social whole.
3. Systems have needs that must be met if they are to survive. Therefore, the function of a structure must be determined by the discovery of the needs that it meets.

The recognition that society was a system made up of interrelated parts was not controversial, but an understanding of how this system functioned in terms of the operation of system parts and system needs were to become the distinctive and highly controversial features of functional analysis. Spencer must be given the credit, or the blame, for explicitly formulating the tenets of modern functionalism. Yet, Spencer himself was not to directly influence modern functionalists in either sociology or anthropology. His utilitarianism lost fashion during the latter part of the last century, as laissez–faire capitalism was being supplanted or supplemented by increased governmental regulation and control. As his star faded in England, Spencer enjoyed a brief period of enormous popularity in America, especially during the early days of social Darwinism.[22] Yet, even in his twilight, Spencer's functionalism was ignored. It was his "law of evolution" and utilitarian concern with "survival of the fittest" that were both his claim to fame and his intellectual undoing.

One of Spencer's harshest critics was Émile Durkheim, the French sociologist and inheritor of the collectivist tradi-

---

[22]*See,* for a readable discussion of Spencer and social Darwinism, Richard Hofstader, *Social Darwinism in American Thought* (Boston: Beacon Press, 1944).

tion of Saint-Simon and Comte. Yet, as we will see, Durkheim borrowed selectively, but heavily, from Spencer. And
in so doing he forged functionalism into a coherent and
acceptable doctrine. We must, therefore, return to France in
the last decade of the 19th century and the early years of
this century in order to complete our review of the emergence of functionalism.

Emile Durkheim and the Codification
of the Functional Orientation

France in Durkheim's time was considerably more stable
than in Comte's. Yet, France was far from tranquil in the
post-revolutionary era. Durkheim thus became concerned
with social order and cohesion, much as had Comte in the
early part of the 19th century. This concern for social stability underlies all of his work, but we must also recognize the
more purely intellectual currents of Durkheim's time.[23] For
convenience we can label these currents the French Tradition and the British Tradition. Each is briefly discussed
below.

ÉMILE DURKHEIM AND THE FRENCH TRADITION
In many respects, Durkheim extended Comte's initial insights. He was, in a sense, the intellectual benefactor of
Saint-Simon's and Comte's work. Durkheim accepted the
general evolutionary theories of his day and Comte's pre-
sumption that laws guide human progress. Durkheim also
embraced Comte's belief that a science of society, based
upon empirical observation, was possible and necessary for
the creation of a better social order. Indeed, Durkheim provided sociology with some of its first examples of sound

---

[23]It is difficult to document precisely all the major influences acting upon
Durkheim's thought as most of his private papers were destroyed. Nisbet, however, has listed some of the scholars that may have influenced him by a direct
examination of Durkheim's works. *See,* in particular, his *The Sociology of Émile
Durkheim* (New York: Oxford, 1974) and his *Émile Durkheim* (Englewood Cliffs,
N.J.: Prentice-Hall). See also Lewis Coser's excellent discussion of Durkheim in
his *Masters of Sociological Thought,* op. cit., pp. 129–174. The most comprehensive
intellectual biography on Durkheim is by Steven Lukes, *Émile Durkheim, His Life
and Work* (London: Allen Lane, 1973). *See also:* D. LaCapra, *Émile Durkheim:
Sociologist and Philosopher* (Ithaca, N.Y.: Cornell University Press, 1972) and
Ernest Wallwork, *Durkheim: Morality and Milieu* (Cambridge, Mass.: Harvard
University Press, 1972).

methodological and statistical analysis.[24] And most important, Durkheim continued the French collectivist tradition with the assertion that society is an emergent reality, *sui generis,* and must therefore be understood in terms of its own unique principles. Echoing Comte's belief that society "can no more be decomposed into individuals than a geometric surface can be resolved into lines, or a line into points,"[25] Durkheim declared:[26] "Society is a reality *sui generis;* it has its own particular characteristics, which are not met with again in the same form in all the rest of the universe. The representations which express it have a wholly different content from purely individual ones." This emphasis on society as an entity in itself dictated for Durkheim a causal analysis of social phenomena that emphasized:[27] "The determining cause of a social fact should not be sought among the states of the individual consciousness."

This was the weight of the French Tradition, as Durkheim accepted and molded it to his purposes. Society is a reality in itself; it is amenable to scientific study; such study must seek the causes of social phenomena in social facts, not individual consciousness; and the study of society, in its broad evolutionary trends, will produce true laws of human organization and change. Implicit in this tradition, of course, is the view that society is an organic whole, or "body social," as Durkheim was often to argue. But the functional implications of this position were not, we contend, originally a part of the French Tradition. Rather, they were borrowed from Spencer, thus supplementing Durkheim's French heritage with ideas from the British Tradition.

ÉMILE DURKHEIM AND THE BRITISH TRADITION
Durkheim's rejection of Spencerian utilitarianism and libertarianism is often viewed as evidence of his dismissal of Spencer's sociology. We must remember, however, that Spencer wore—rather uncomfortably, it must be empha-

---

[24]*See,* in particular, Durkheim's *The Rules of the Sociological Method* (New York: Free Press, 1938, original 1895); *The Division of Labor in Society* (New York: Free Press, 1933, original 1893); and *Suicide* (New York: Free Press, 1951, original 1897).

[25]Comte, in Levy-Bruhl's translation, op. cit., p. 258.

[26]Quoted from Nisbet, *Émile Durkheim,* op. cit., p. 33.

[27]*Rules of the Sociological Method,* op. cit., p. 110.

sized—two intellectual hats. On the one side was Spencer's staunch utilitarian philosophy as it became translated in libertarian doctrines and social Darwinism. And, on the other side, was Spencer's organicism as it developed into the law of evolution, the organismic analogy, and a concern with structure and function.

Most of this latter tradition Durkheim embraced. His criticism of Spencer's work is wholly against utilitarianism and its failure to recognize that social exchanges in the marketplace and elsewhere have a moral component and are guided by cultural ideas. Moreover, Durkheim was repulsed by the tendency of Spencer to view society, when wearing his utilitarian hat, as the mere "sum of individuals."[28] But there can be little doubt that Durkheim read Spencer's *Principles of Sociology* very closely[29] and that his functional approach was, in good part, shaped by Spencerian sociology.

ÉMILE DURKHEIM'S FUNCTIONAL ORIENTATION
The coalescence of the French and British Traditions, as they were synthesized in Durkheim's creative mind, created the functional orientation. Durkheim first borrowed Spencer's distinction between structure and function. He argued that it is useful to ask the question: What is the function for the "body social" of a particular structure? For example, in his first important work, *The Division of Labor in Society,* Durkheim asked: What is the function of the division of labor for society? In such a question there is an implicit notion, which Durkheim also borrowed from Spencer, that in order to answer the question it is necessary to have some notion of the "needs" of society. That is, what does a society need to survive? Durkheim's answer was clearly in the French Tradition: a society must be integrated, or reveal solidarity among its component parts. Thus, most of Durkheim's work concerned the analysis of

[28]It should be emphasized that in his personal life Durkheim was as libertarian and individualistic as Spencer. Yet, Durkheim's fear of a repressive state destroying individual freedom was not as evident in his formal writings as it was in Spencer's.

[29]There are 40 references to Spencer in *The Division of Labor* alone. It should be mentioned also that Spencer influenced many of Durkheim's evolutionary ideas. For example, it was Spencer who had first conceptualized in analytic detail the movement of societies from a state of homogeneity to a state of heterogeneity.

how a given structure meets the integrative needs of society. In *The Division of Labor,* for example, Durkheim discovered that the division of labor provides a new basis of solidarity in rapidly differentiating societies. And to the degree that this need for solidarity is not met by the division of labor, "pathological" states like "anomie" are likely to occur.

Thus far, we can see that Durkheim codified Spencer's distinction of structure and function into a clear mode of analysis. Moreover, unlike Spencer,[30] Durkheim used this mode of analysis in a number of empirical studies, such as *The Division of Labor in Society* and *The Elementary Forms of the Religious Life.* We will shortly illustrate with these two classic studies the full significance of Durkheim's functionalism.

In his functional analysis Durkheim recognized a potential problem. This is the problem of illegitimate teleology, to which we will return in later chapters. For now, we can state the problem as Durkheim saw it. To discover the "need" that a structure "functions" to meet does *not* necessarily reveal its cause—that is, the sequence of events that created the structure in the first place. To do so would assume that "need" for a structure causes it to emerge, which is to "put the cart before the horse." How, for example, does a need for solidarity cause a division of labor to emerge? In other words, how can the results of an event be its cause? This problem led Durkheim to emphasize:[31]

> To show how a fact is useful is not to explain how it originated or why it is what it is. . . . The need we have of things cannot give them existence, nor can it confer their specific nature upon them. It is to causes of another sort that they owe their existence . . . [for] no force can be engendered except by an antecedent force.

This is a critical line of argument, for it introduces a new distinction to the emerging functional orientation: functional and causal analysis must be separated. Causal analysis asks: Why does the structure in question exist and reveal certain properties? Functional analysis asks: What need of

[30]In contrast to Spencer's use of data which was selective and self-serving, Durkheim's analysis of data was a welcome departure from Spencer.

[31]*The Rules,* op. cit., p. 90.

the larger system does the structure meet? To confuse the two questions is to invite an illegitimate teleology[32] where consequences cause the events producing them. Thus, Durkheim emphasizes that the causes of social phenomena must be distinguished from the ends that they serve:[33]

> When, then, the explanation of a social phenomenon is undertaken, we must seek separately the efficient cause which produces it and the function it fulfills. We use the word "function" in preference to "end" or "purpose," precisely because social phenomena do not generally exist for the useful results they produce.

This distinction between cause and function owes its origin to Durkheim's French heritage. On the one hand, Durkheim followed Comte's pleas for an objective science of society, because an analysis of cause and effect would uncover the laws of human organization. On the other hand, Durkheim, like Comte, Saint-Simon, and other French thinkers, was a moralist: He wanted to create the "good" society. Functional analysis thus has its origins in the perpetual dilemma facing most social scientists: objective analysis of events and a desire to create a better society.

While Durkheim's mandate that causal and functional analysis be separate is praiseworthy, it is a distinction that is often difficult to maintain in actual practice. As we will see in our examination of many functionalists' work in the pages to follow, cause and function are not easily separated. They often become subtly confused, creating a host of moral, substantive, and logical problems for "the science of society."

We should anticipate some of these problems by reviewing briefly the arguments in Durkheim's two great functional works, *The Division of Labor in Society* and *The Elementary Forms of the Religious Life.* Here, in the actual application of a functional orientation, we can begin to see problems that seem remote in an abstract discussion.

The Division of Labor in Society   Figure 1.1 represents Durkheim's argument in *The Division of Labor,* his first

---

[32]This is not always the case, as we will explore in a later chapter.
[33]*The Rules,* op. cit., p. 96.

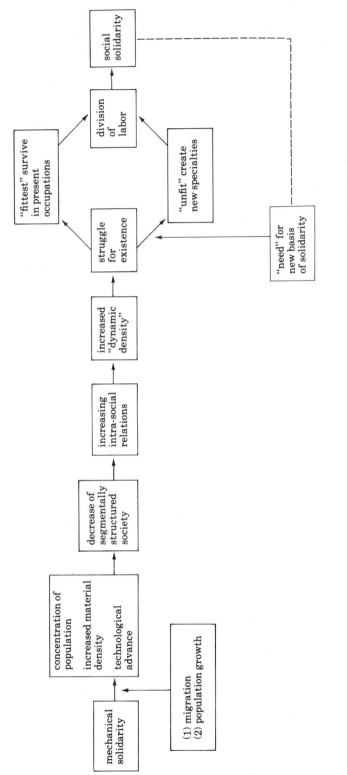

------- = implied teleology

FIGURE 1.1 Durkheim's Casual Model for the Division of Labor

important work.[34] Like Comte, Spencer, and many others, Durkheim observed that societies develop from simple, undifferentiated "mechanical" societies to complex, highly differentiated "organic" societies. Simple societies are based upon the likeness of their parts, complex ones on differences. In simple societies, a common system of values, beliefs, and norms—what Durkheim termed "the collective conscience"—regulates social affairs. In more complex societies, however, differences in system parts "require" additional mechanisms of integration. It becomes increasingly difficult, Durkheim observed, to integrate with a common idea system–wide varieties of occupations located in the separated institutions—government, law, family, religion, community, education, and economy. In traditional societies the diversity of occupations is less; and for the most part, activity is carried out within the institution of kinship. Distinctive and separate institutions of government, economy, and education do not become highly differentiated from kinship, and thus integration and social cohesion can be maintained by acceptance of, and adherence to, one common idea system.

Durkheim emphasized that the trends toward industrialization in France, and the resulting occupational specialization, urbanization, and proliferation of roles in separate governmental, legal, educational, and religious institutions, were part of this grand evolutionary trend—of the movement from societies based upon mechanical solidarity to those based on organic solidarity. Durkheim asked two basic questions in *The Division of Labor:* What caused the movement from mechanical to organic societies? And, what are the functions of the proliferating division of labor? His answer to this last question was, of course, predictable: the division of labor promotes social solidarity, or in other words, provides a new basis for social integration in differentiated societies.

Durkheim's causal analysis occupies most of Figure 1.1. Migration and population growth, coupled with new technologies such as transportation and communication systems, increase the number of potential relations in the society. Population growth and the resulting increase in

---

[34]Originally published in 1893.

social relations escalates the level of "dynamic density"—that is the number and variety of contacts among people. Such a situation typically leads to conflict over limited resources, with the result that occupational specialization occurs among those with varying levels of ability. The result is the division of labor which makes people interdependent upon each other, and along with broad cultural values and beliefs, provides a new basis for social integration.

As can be seen, much of Durkheim's argument is borrowed from Spencer. Population increases escalate the levels of competition, with the abilities of those in the competition determining their social niche in the division of labor. The causal imagery is also as vague as that attributed by Durkheim to Spencer: How and why is competition increased? How and why does competition lead to a division of labor? One answer is a functional one: The division of labor is created because it is needed. Social systems must be integrated, and thus the "need" for a new basis of integration "causes" the "struggle for existence" to be transformed into a division of labor.

This is a critical point, for now Durkheim has undone his carefully drawn distinction between causal and functional analysis. The "need for" a division of labor, or the "functions" it is to fulfill, are involved in ways that go unspecified in the causes of the division of labor. Here, we can see in concrete terms the problem of illegitimate teleology—of a situation where an end state like the division of labor causes the events leading to that end, without any specification of how this is so. We will not dwell on the problem until later chapters, except to emphasize that there is often great difficulty in functional analysis of keeping causal and functional statements separated. Durkheim's analysis of the division of labor is a classic illustration of this problem, and if Durkheim failed to keep cause and function distinct, then it is not surprising that others who followed him have fallen into the same intellectual trap.

The Analysis of Religion   As with his analysis of the division of labor in 1893, Durkheim's last major work in 1912, *The Elementary Forms of the Religious Life,* [35] sought to un-

---

[35] *The Elementary Forms of the Religious Life* (New York: Free Press, 1948). Originally published in 1912 and first translated into English in 1915.

cover the causes and functions of religion. Durkheim had been preoccupied with religion throughout his career, but it was not until 1912 that he pulled his ideas together into a synthetic statement.[36] Durkheim's lifelong interest in religion can be traced to his moral concern with bringing social order to society. Religion had been throughout human history one of the "great regulating functions of society." Therefore, if he could uncover why and how religion provided integration, then it might be possible to use this knowledge to integrate his own society.[37]

Durkheim's analysis of religion focused on its "elementary forms" for a simple reason: By looking at religion in its simplest form, many of the distracting complexities of religion in developed societies could be eliminated. This strategy followed from a critical assumption: Religion in all societies, both simple and advanced, serves the *same* function, and therefore, this function could more easily be determined in a simple than in a complex society. Durkheim recognized that while religion greatly increases in its complexity with societal development, it nevertheless serves essentially the same function. As he noted,[38] "All religions serve the same needs ..., the different totems of the tribe fulfill exactly the same functions that will later fall upon the divine personalities."

What is this function? For Durkheim, the answer is predictable: religion provides a basis for the integration of society. It unites people into a common system of ideas which then regulates their affairs. It is thus with this conclusion about the functions of religion, and with the strategy of focusing on the simplest or "elementary" of its forms, that Durkheim began his analysis of religion.

Durkheim defined religious phenomena as consisting of (1) beliefs about a supernatural and sacred realm, and (2) rites and rituals directed toward this realm. He then turned

[36]See Lukes, op. cit, for the best statement on Durkheim's long-term interest in morality and religion.

[37]Durkheim was heavily influenced by Comte. He saw the force of religion declining in his day and wanted to substitute a "civil religion" as a substitute, although not of the type advocated by Comte's teacher, Saint-Simon. In this belief, he was implicitly following Comte's law of the three stages, where the religious stage is eventually replaced by positivism—that is, the use of empirically based knowledge to organize society. This is, we feel, the source of Durkheim's long-term interest in religion.

[38]*Elementary Forms,* op. cit., p. 179.

to the detailed, and terribly flawed and ethnocentric, analysis of religion among Australian aboriginals, most particularly the Arunta people.[39] He chose these people because in his view no human society could be more simply structured and, therefore, their religions could not be explained as the result of earlier religious forms. Durkheim thus believed that the aboriginals represented a pristine "case study" of the first human societies.[40]

Durkheim's description of the social structure of the aboriginal tribes led him to note that all the tribes have certain common features: (1) Each tribe is divided into a number of clans, or large kinship networks; (2) each of the clans that together form a tribe has its own totem, with associated rituals; and (3) each totem reveals sacred symbols, particularly a special plant or animal which is represented in an emblem. Durkheim thus saw the aboriginals as divided into clans, with each clan revealing a totem symbolized by sacred objects. For Durkheim, such a structure was the most "elementary form of religion." He then set out to discover what causes the emergence of this elementary form and what its functions are for the aboriginal tribes. As we know, the functional analysis was a foregone conclusion, but the causal analysis is rarely discussed in commentaries, particularly the relation of his causal statements to his functional argument.

In Figure 1.2, we have sought to diagram this relationship. Our discussion will move from the left side of the diagram, outlining his purely causal argument, to the right side of the figure where causal and functional arguments become intertwined. Durkheim believed that presocietal humans wandered over their territories, occasionally coming together. During such gatherings a kind of crowd behavior occurred in which the contact with others produced heightened stimulation, or in his words, "awakened passions."[41] During this state, people become sensitized to each

---

[39]Durkheim's use of ethnographies—themselves highly inaccurate—was no less ethnocentric and self-serving than Spencer's. It was in statistical analysis, and methodological sophistication, that Durkheim surpassed his peers.

[40]Durkheim never abandoned his evolutionary perspective. He saw religion as developing from simple to complex forms—as did Spencer.

[41]Durkheim appears to be drawing much from Gustav Le Bon, and even his intellectual enemy, Gabriel Tarde, scholars whom he had rather mercilessly dismissed in his early work, *Suicide,* op. cit.

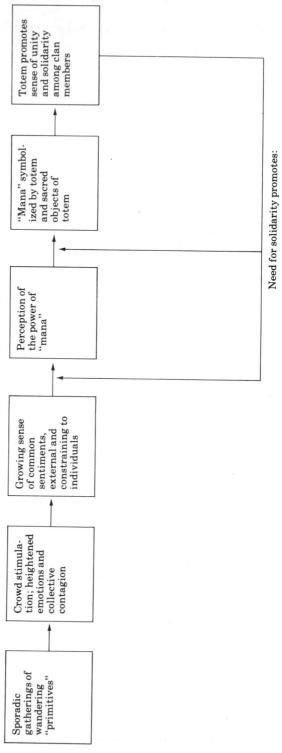

FIGURE 1.2 Durkheim's Causal and Functional Argument for the Emergence of Religion

other's feelings and emotions, with the combined force of sentiments appearing like an external force on individuals. In his words,[42]

> There are at once transports of enthusiasm. In the contrary conditions, he is to be seen running here and there like a madman, giving himself up to all sorts of immoderate movements, crying, shrieking, rolling in the dust, throwing it in every direction, biting himself, brandishing his arms in a furious manner, etc. The very fact of the concentration acts as an exceptionally powerful stimulant. When they are once come together, a sort of electricity is formed by their collecting which quickly transports them to an extraordinary degree of exaltation. Every sentiment expressed finds a place without resistance in all the minds, which are very open to outside impressions; each re-echoes the others, and is re-echoed by the others. The initial impulse thus proceeds, growing as it goes, as an avalanche grows in its advance ... And since a collective sentiment cannot express itself collectively except on the condition of observing a certain order permitting co-operation and movements in unison, these gestures and cries naturally tend to become rhythmic and regular; hence come songs and dances. But in taking a more regular form, they lose nothing of their natural violence; a regulated tumult remains.

This developing "collective conscience" increasingly appears as a powerful force, external to individuals. At some point, this force is seen as "mana"—strong and diffuse powers that exist in the supernatural, extraordinary realm. But this power, Durkheim felt, needed to be explained; strong and powerful sentiments needed to be attached to a visible and concrete object. Hence, animal or plants, symbolized in emblems, become the concrete objects that represent and personify "mana." As Durkheim noted:[43] "Totemism is the religion not of such and such animals or men or images, but of an anonymous and impersonal force, found in each of these beings but not to be confounded with any of them...." And as he emphasized:[44] " ... religious force is nothing other than the collective and anonymous force of the clan, and since this can be represented in mind only in the form

[42]*Elementary Forms,* op. cit., pp. 246–247.
[43]Ibid., p. 217.
[44]Ibid., p. 253.

of the totem, the totemic emblem is like the visible body of god."

This was, at the time and perhaps even today, a startling conclusion.[45] Religious beliefs symbolize society; and ritual directed toward the sacred entities that are contained in these beliefs represents the worship of society itself. It is at this juncture that we should note how the functional and causal analysis become confounded. As the hidden worship of society itself, religion provides its members with a common set of ideas which commits them to the society. It thus serves integrative functions, or meets the "need for" social solidarity. We can now ask, as Durkheim explicitly did, what causes aroused collectives who "feel the presence of mana" to create totems? Durkheim's message was clear: The need for social solidarity causes emotionally aroused collectivities of humans to create totems. Here again there is the possibility of an illegitimate teleology: the end result —the need for social solidarity—causes the event—religion —that meets this end. Without more precise statements as to how, why, and through what specific processes this need causes religion, the causal argument becomes an illegitimate teleology.

DURKHEIM IN REVIEW: HIS SIGNIFICANCE FOR FUNCTIONAL ANALYSIS

As we have noted, Durkheim codified the functional approach, drawing heavily from Spencer. His carefully drawn distinction between cause and function, when coupled with Spencer's separation of structure and function, presented sociology and anthropology with the basic elements of the functional orientation. We have emphasized some of the problems with these distinctions as Durkheim undertook the detailed analysis of the division of labor and the elementary forms of religion. These will be discussed extensively, as we proceed to explore the development of the functional orientation.

We have concentrated on these two empirical investigations for yet another reason. Each was to influence the next

---

[45]However, this basic idea was not original with Durkheim. Roberston Smith and his followers had already seen this basic connection between religion and society. For a more detailed account of Durkheim's debt to Smith, see Lukes, op. cit.

generation of functional theorists in sociology and anthropology. Particularly in anthropology, Durkheim's functional analysis of religion was to stimulate the two great anthropologists, A. R. Radcliffe-Brown and Bronislaw Malinowski, the subjects of the next chapter. And, as we shall later see, these anthropologists, by keeping alive functionalism, were to encourage the development of sociological functionalism, the topic of Chapter 4.

2

The Preservation of Functionalism

Except for a rather remarkable set of circumstances, functionalism probably would have died with Durkheim. We must keep in mind that at the turn of the century Durkheim was virtually unknown to American audiences. His work remained untranslated until well into the 20th century; and particularly among American sociologists, his ideas had little impact until 1937, when Talcott Parsons, who eventually was to carry functional thought to its culmination, published his first major work, *The Structure of Social Action.*[1] Yet, even in this work, Durkheim's functionalism is not discussed. And neither is Spencer's, for indeed the book opens with the question, "Who now reads Spencer?" and proceeds to show why the rejection of Spencer's sociology was justified.

In light of the general ignorance of Spencer's and Durkheim's work, how and why did functionalism survive? How did the work of an untranslated scholar in France come to have such an impact on British and American social science, particularly sociology and anthropology? The answer to these questions resides in the intellectual environment of England during the first decades of the 20th century and in the efforts of two charismatic scholars, A. R. Radcliffe-Brown and Bronislaw Malinowski, to redirect anthropological thinking. Functionalism, then, persisted not

[1] Talcott Parsons, *The Structure of Social Action* (New York: McGraw-Hill, 1937).

in sociology but in anthropology and only later became part of the sociological tradition.[2] Our goal in this chapter, therefore, is to seek an understanding of why Durkheim's functional thought was preserved in the anthropological tradition and elaborated by Radcliffe-Brown and Malinowski into modern functionalism.

The Intellectual Milieu of Early Anthropology

Functionalism was a reaction to, and resolution for, the intellectual problems and debates of early anthropology. To appreciate these problems, we should try to visualize the world of the 19th–century and early 20th–century anthropologist: travelers, missionaries, explorers, and amateur anthropologists have been collecting "data" on the "primitive" and "savage" peoples that they have encountered. Imagine the impact of tales about the aborigines in Australia, the bands and tribes of Africa, and the Indian cultures of the Americas on the scholars of Victorian England and on the European continent. What are they to do with the mass of ethnographic "data" that is accumulating? How are they to organize it and to give it interpretation? Three answers, each in its own way to prove unsatisfactory, were advanced: (1) evolutionism, (2) diffusionism, and (3) historicism, or historical reconstruction. It is out of the inadequacies of these approaches that functionalism was reborn and elaborated.

EVOLUTIONISM
As we emphasized in the last chapter, the Darwinian theory of evolution had been an intellectual bombshell, not just in biology but also in the social sciences. It was perhaps a natural intellectual tendency to apply evolutionary notions to the mounds of accumulating data. There was, of course, ample intellectual precedent for the application of evolutionary ideas to the social realm. As we saw, Comte, Spencer, and Durkheim all viewed human organization as moving from simple to complex forms. The movement of society from simple to complex, however, represented a

[2]*See:* Jonathan H. Turner, *The Structure of Sociological Theory* (Homewood, Ill.: Dorsey Press, 1974).

gross distortion of Darwin's theory. For as Robert Nisbet[3] has so forcefully pointed out, the metaphor of progress—that is, of perpetual betterment—has permeated Western social thought from the time of the Greeks, and nowhere is the power of this metaphor more evident than in 19th–century doctrines of social evolution.

Basically, social evolutionism held that humankind was evolving along a single path culminating, not surprisingly, in Western European civilization.[4] All societies—from the simplest aboriginal to the most industrial—could be pegged at a particular stage of evolutionary development. The task of the anthropologist thus became one of discovering the stage of development in a society, and then with the use of the comparative method, placing it with others of its kind at the proper point in the evolutionary scale.

In retrospect this kind of thinking seems, at best, to be naive, and at worst, to be supportive of colonialism and racism (since, after all, black populations were at the bottom and white populations at the top of the evolutionary scale). Yet, evolutionism resulted in one important accomplishment: It planted in the anthropological imagination the idea that the wealth of accumulating data on "primitive peoples" could be organized and understood by an overarching intellectual scheme.

DIFFUSIONISM

As the inadequacies of evolutionism increasingly became evident, the doctrine of diffusionism was substituted for evolutionism.[5] This doctrine held that "anthropological

[3]Robert A. Nisbet, *Social Change and History* (New York: Oxford University Press, 1969).

[4]Some of the early leaders of the evolutionary school included: H. S. Maine, *Ancient Law* (London: J. Murray, 1861); H. Spencer, *The Study of Sociology* (New York: D. Appleton, 1873) and *Principles of Sociology* (New York: D. Appleton, 1896, original 1876); L. H. Morgan, *Ancient Society*. E. Leacock, ed. (New York: Meridian Books: World Publishing, 1963, original 1877); Edward B. Tylor, *Researches into the Early History of Mankind and the Development of Civilization* (London: J. Murray, 1964, original 1865), and *The Origins of Culture* (New York: Harper and Row, 1958, originally published as Chapter IX of *Primitive Culture* in 1871); J. G. Frazer, *The Golden Bough* (New York: Macmillan, 1958, original 1890).

[5]Prominent diffusionists in the German and English schools include: in Germany, F. Ratzel, *The History of Mankind*. A. J. Butler, trans. (London: Macmillan 1896–1898); Fritz Graebner, *Methode der Ethnologie* (Heidelberg: Carl Winter's Universitätsbuchhandlung, 1911); W. Schmitt, *The Culture Historical Method of Ethnology*. S. A. Suber, trans. (New York: Fortuny's, 1939); and in England, W. H. R. Rivers, *The History of Melanesian Society* (Cambridge: Cambridge University Press, 1914); G. E. Smith, *In the Beginning: The Origin of Civilization* (New York: Morrow, 1928).

traits tend to diffuse in all directions from their centers of origin."[6] Thus, the argument ran, there are cultural centers from which traits radiate and which are then adopted by societies distant from these centers. In its most extreme form, the diffusionists argued that there was but one cultural center from which traits had diffused all over the world. For example, Eliot Smith[7] developed a scheme during the early decades of this century that had the entire cultural inventory of the earth emanating from ancient Egypt.

The deficiencies of diffusionism soon became evident, although the dialogue between Smith and other diffusionists on the one side and the functionalists, Radcliffe-Brown and Malinowski on the other side raged for decades. But the obvious fact of independent discovery and invention and of the isolation of cultures from each other eventually made diffusionism as unappealing as evolutionism. Yet, diffusionism did have several important consequences: The diffusionists helped destroy the naive evolutionism of early anthropology and they focused attention on the traits of particular cultures.

HISTORICISM AND HISTORICAL RECONSTRUCTION

In America, Franz Boas was launching devastating critiques against evolutionism, and to a lesser extent, against diffusionism. He did not, of course, reject the general notions that societies evolve and change or that they borrow traits from each other. Rather, he found intolerable the extremes of both the evolutionists' and diffusionists' positions.[8]

Boas argued that each culture must be viewed as an entity in itself. Idle speculation about a particular society's place on some evolutionary scale was a waste of intellectual energy, as were blanket assertions about the diffusion of traits from cultural centers. Instead, the anthropologist must ex-

---

[6]C. Wissler, *The Relation of Nature to Man in Aboriginal America* (New York: Oxford University Press, 1926), p. 183.

[7]Eliot G. Smith, *In the Beginning: The Origin of Civilization* (New York: Morrow, 1928); *The Diffusion of Culture* (London: Watts, 1933).

[8]Franz Boas, "The Limitations of the Comparative Method of Anthropology" in *Race, Language and Culture* (New York: Macmillan, 1940) pp. 271–304. (It is often noted that this work coincided with the demise of the evolutionary method in America.) In fact, Boas began his studies under the evolutionary paradigm, only later coming to reject the implied racism of his practitioners.

amine, describe, and record the characteristics of each society, while seeking to reconstruct the historical events that led to the emergence of these characteristics.

Boas realized that most traditional societies of the world were fast disappearing, and he argued that a body of facts about the historical record of each unique culture is essential to the development of theory. He thus sent his students —the first generation of prominent American anthropologists—Alfred Kroeber, Edward Sapir, Ruth Benedict, Alexander Lesser, and Robert Lowie, to name but a few—into the field to describe and to reconstruct the history of the world's vanishing traditional societies.

Boas' method of historical reconstruction proved to be hard to execute, since traditional societies do not have written or accurate verbal records of their past. But his emphasis on the uniqueness of each society, to be understood in terms of itself rather than in regard to its stage in any evolutionary hierarchy or its acquisition of traits from a cultural center, represented a needed and important departure from previous modes of anthropological thinking. Moreover, this emphasis on the individual society and its internal operation paralleled the emerging functional orientation of Malinowski and Radcliffe-Brown.[9]

The Rise of Anthropological Functionalism

If cultures are not to be viewed as stages of evolution or as recipients of traits from cultural centers, and if the task of the anthropologist is to describe the character and reconstruct the unique history of each society, then the intellectual problems that spawned evolutionism and diffusionism re-emerge. How is all the ethnographic data to be interpreted? And how is the individual field worker in a strange and alien world to make sense of each cultural trait?

These questions were implicitly asked by Durkheim in his *The Elementary Forms of the Religious Life.* Here, as we saw in the last chapter, Durkheim analyzed cultural traits, particularly religious rituals, in terms of their consequences for social integration. The concept of function thus

---

[9]Some have argued that Boas was a functionalist. This argument, we feel, is not correct, for Boas did not invoke notions of function, or system needs and requisites. He did, however, view cultures as social wholes of interconnected parts.

gave Durkheim a "handle" on the collage of traits possessed by Australian aboriginals. If the function of a trait could be discovered, then its place in the broader society could now be "understood." And if traits in different societies could also be seen to perform similar functions, then even greater understanding of patterns of human organization could be achieved.

Durkheim said all of this in 1912, the publication date of *The Elementary Forms of the Religious Life*.[10] He had, of course, made his functional approach explicit much earlier[11] in *The Division of Labor in Society* (1893) and *The Rules of the Sociological Method* (1895). Radcliffe-Brown and Malinowski had clearly read these latter works in the original French, but coincidentally they had also been performing analyses of Australian aboriginals at the same time as Durkheim. As a footnote, it should be noted that Sigmund Freud was also preparing his classic, *Totem and Taboo*,[12] from the same data source on Australian aborigines. We have, then, a convergence of interest among four of the social sciences' greatest intellects. Durkheim and Freud were preparing analyses of religion while Malinowski and Radcliffe-Brown were analyzing kinship among the aborigines. All of these scholars are, as can best be discerned, unaware of each other's efforts.[13] And thus, in 1912 and 1913, four separate analyses of Australian aborigines emanate from the pens of these great scholars.

Anthropologists soon became aware of Durkheim's analysis of religion, and indeed, Malinowski performed a critical book review of Durkheim's last great work.[14] What is important is that Durkheim's sojourn into primitive culture

[10]Émile Durkheim, *The Elementary Forms of the Religious Life* (New York: Free Press, 1915, originally published 1912).

[11]Émile Durkheim, *The Division of Labor in Society* (New York: Free Press, 1933, originally published in 1893), *The Rules of the Sociological Method* (New York: Free Press, 1938, originally published in 1895); and *Suicide* (New York: Free Press, 1951, originally published in 1897).

[12]Sigmund Freud, *Totem and Taboo* (London: Penguin Books, 1938, original 1913).

[13]As best as we can determine, three of these scholars were relying on the same compilation of ethnographic data by Baldwin Spencer and F. J. Gillen, *The Native Tribes of Central Australia* (London: Macmillan, 1899) and *The Northern Tribes of Central Australia* (London: Macmillan, 1904). Radcliffe-Brown, however, conducted his own field work in Australia between 1910 and 1912.

[14]Bronislaw Malinowski, review of *Les Formers Élémentaires De La Vie Religieuse* in *Folklore*, 24 (1913):525–531.

probably rekindled interest among anthropologists in his thinking. For by application of his functional approach to societies of interest to anthropologists, he converted Radcliffe-Brown and Malinowski to his approach, and in so doing, he assured the dominance of the functional approach in 20th–century anthropology and sociology.

This line of argument is buttressed by a letter written to Radcliffe-Brown by Émile Durkheim on November 9, 1913:

> Dear Sir:
> Absent from Paris since the beginning of August, I found your booklet only on my return some days ago; it waited for me at home like all books and printed matter. This explains to you my involuntary delay in acknowledging its receipt and in thanking you for the kind letter which accompanied it.
> I am grateful for the opportunity that you have thus offered me of entering into direct relations with you and I am extremely glad to learn from you that we are in agreement concerning the general principles of the science [sociology]. Nothing could have given me greater confidence in the method that I am trying to apply.

Moreover, J. G. Peristiany, who received this letter personally from Radcliffe-Brown shortly before the latter's death, noted that all those who came into close contact with Radcliffe-Brown "know that he considered Durkheim one of his masters, and this is certainly apparent in the best of his writings. The care with which this letter was preserved in his annotated copy of Durkheim's *Le Suicide* shows his reverence for the older man" (Peristiany, 1960:318–319).[15]

The growing fascination of anthropologists with functionalism is also revealed in Malinowski's *The Family among the Australian Aborigines,* his first major work published in 1913.[16] For the most part, the book is concerned with the basis of authority within the family and it follows the traditional evolutionary and diffusionist approach primarily because it was written under the influence of such

---

[15]Apparently there was no further correspondence between the two men. World War I broke out the following year and Durkheim, despondent over the death of his son, died before the war ended. The booklet referred to in the letter was: A. R. Brown, "Three Tribes of Western Australia," *Journal of Royal Anthropological Institute of Great Britain and Ireland,* XLIII (1913). (At this time, Radcliffe-Brown went by the name, A. R. Brown.)

[16]B. Malinowski, *The Family among the Australian Aborigines* (New York: Schocken, 1963, originally published 1913).

British scholars as Frazer, Seligman, Rivers, and Wester-marck. Yet the book has frequent references to Durkheim. And, in the closing pages of this work one can see the incipi-ent beginnings of Malinowski's later commitment to the analysis of institutions in terms of their functions:[17]

> Social institutions should in the first place be defined by their social functions; . . . of the functions . . . known and compared . . . each of these institutions will appear as occupying a defi-nite place in the social organization, and playing a determi-nate part in the life of the community.[18]

The adoption of Durkheim's functional approach must also be viewed in the intellectual context of Radcliffe-Brown's and Malinowski's time. They had been trained by British diffusionists, and thus, had certainly been told of the deficiencies of evolutionism. Moreover, they were among the first anthropologists to perform detailed and systematic field work on traditional societies—Malinowski[19] in the Trobriand Islands (1915–1918) and Radcliffe-Brown[20] in the Andaman Islands (1906–1908). Indeed, Malinowski's fa-mous ethnography on the Trobriand Islanders still stands as a model for contemporary field research.[21] They had thus discovered, first hand, the problems of reconstructing the past among peoples who had no historical records and of trying to visualize tiny island societies as recipients of traits from Egypt or some other cultural center.

In this intellectual vacuum, then, they faced that nagging question: How were they, or others, to make sense of the traits of traditional peoples? Durkheim's answer must have

[17]Since most of the book is not concerned with function (Malinowski began the book in Poland before 1910), it can be guessed that by the time he wrote the last few pages he had read Durkheim's *Elementary Forms.*

[18]Malinowski, *The Family . . .,* op. cit., p. 303.

[19]Malinowski's Trobriand ethnography is contained in five books: *The Sexual Life of Savages* (vol. I and II, New York: Horace Liveright, 1929); *Coral Gardens and Their Magic* (New York: American Book Company, 1935); *Crime and Custom in Savage Society* (New York: The Humanities Press, Inc., 1951, original 1926); *Argonauts of the Western Pacific* (New York: E. P. Dutton, 1961, original 1922); and *The Language of Magic and Gardening* (Bloomington: Indiana University Press, 1965, original 1935).

[20]A. R. Radcliffe-Brown, *The Andaman Islanders* (Glencoe, Ill.: Free Press, 1948, first edition 1922).

[21]To this day Malinowski's ethnography is often cited as the most complete and well-done study of an aboriginal society. Indeed it was he who pioneered the participant-observation method, being the first professional anthropologist to pitch his tent and live entirely with the people he was studying.

had a special appeal to these pioneer field researchers: Assess the function of a cultural item. By knowing the functions of a cultural item—be it a religious ritual, a kinship system, or some other trait—its place in the overall scheme of things could be known. Such was the appeal of Durkheim's functional approach. And it is this appeal that assured the preservation of functionalism. For without the combination of circumstances that we have just explored, it is doubtful that functional theorizing would have persisted in the social sciences.

We are now in a position to explore in more detail how Radcliffe-Brown and Malinowski adopted, and then adapted to their purposes, Durkheim's functionalism. As we will come to see, Radcliffe-Brown's approach was much less elaborate and had considerably more influence on anthropology than Malinowski's functional approach. Yet, it is Malinowski who developed a functional scheme that was to lay the foundation for sociological functionalism.

A. R. Radcliffe-Brown and the Preservation of Functionalism

A. R. Radcliffe-Brown (1881–1955) was one of anthropology's most respected and important scholars. He enjoyed enormous professional popularity during his career, and continues to be held in high esteem today. Much of Radcliffe-Brown's popularity stems from his keen and open mind as well as from his world travels across five continents.[22] His written works are relatively few, especially for a scholar of his stature, but his influence was often informal, stemming from his classroom lectures or from his seminars and debates with colleagues.

While Radcliffe-Brown had read Durkheim's *The Division of Labor* and *The Rules of the Sociological Method* during his graduate studies, he appears to have embraced functionalism only after confronting the problems of field

[22]Radcliffe–Brown spent the years 1906–1908 in the Andaman Islands, 1910–1912 in Australia, World War I in Tonga, 1922–1925 in South Africa, 1926–1930 in Australia, 1931–1937 in America. In 1937 he returned to England, but spent much of World War II in Brazil, Asia, and Africa. After retirement, he went to Cairo, Egypt, and later to Grahamstown, South Africa. In all these and other places, he helped establish and build anthropology programs.

work among traditional peoples. His first published work—
the 1913 analysis of kinship among the Australian aborigines—does not reveal any functional theorizing.[23] Yet, there
is clear evidence that Radcliffe-Brown was having great
difficulty employing the diffusionist model of his mentors
and the method of historical reconstruction advocated by
Boas in America. Repeatedly, he remarks on the impossibility of discovering what transpired in the historical past of
the aborigines. It is apparent, then, that the young Radcliffe-Brown (at this time, writing under the name A. R.
Brown) had begun to encounter the problems of employing
the dominant approaches of his day—a fact which was to
make him highly receptive to Durkheim's functionalism.

Radcliffe-Brown's first ethnographic study on the Andaman Islands was conducted from 1906 to 1908. However,
this early study was not published until 1922; and by this
time, his disenchantment with historical reconstruction,
evolutionism, and diffusionism led him to embrace functionalism.[24] The delayed publication of his *The Andaman
Islanders*[25] in 1922 marked a dramatic point in the history
of functionalism. For in this ethnography Radcliffe-Brown
had adopted much of Durkheim's functional method. From
this point on, Radcliffe-Brown's work revealed a clear functional bent, although not to the degree evident in the work
of his colleague and frequent protagonist, Bronislaw Malinowski.

Shortly after the publication of *The Andaman Islanders,*
Radcliffe–Brown published a classic article on the "mother's brother" in certain South African tribes.[26] Here, he
takes to task previous historical and evolutionary interpretations of kinship relations, and in the place of these earlier
interpretations he offers a decidedly functional explanation.

By 1924, then, Radcliffe–Brown's commitment to the
functional approach of Durkheim was clear. As he traveled,
lectured, and wrote, the contours of this approach became

[23]"Three Tribes of Western Australia," op. cit.

[24]Radcliffe–Brown had, of course, become familiar with the incipient functionalism of Malinowski's *The Family Among the Australian Aborigines,* op. cit.,
performing a review of this work in *Man,* 14 (1914):31–32.

[25]Op. cit.

[26]"The Mother's Brother in South Africa," *South African Journal of Science,*
XXI (1924).

increasingly evident. Much of his approach remained un-published until after his death while other of his writings were lodged in obscure journals. Yet, Radcliffe-Brown's work, both published and unpublished, influenced an en-tire generation of anthropologists. His methods for the analysis of kinship are still used. And most important, he gave a generation of anthropologists all over the world a method that they could use in collecting ethnographic data on traditional peoples. Since Radcliffe-Brown's influence extended way beyond his formal publications, our analysis of his functionalism will treat his work—both published and unpublished—from 1922 to 1940 as a whole. In this way we can appreciate what his students saw in his functional approach. For Radcliffe-Brown provided anthropologists, who were committed to the collection of field data, with a mode of analysis that represented an alternative to evolu-tionism, historicism, and diffusionism. The discussion will be organized into several topics: (1) Radcliffe-Brown's view of science, (2) his conception of social structure, (3) his com-mitment to synchronic analysis, and (4) his use of the con-cept of function.

RADCLIFFE-BROWN'S VIEW OF SCIENCE

Unlike most social scientists of his time, or even today, Rad-cliffe-Brown was well versed in philosophy and in the way science was conducted in other disciplines. His most elo-quent statement on the social sciences was given in 1937 before a faculty seminar at the University of Chicago (the transcripts of which were later published in 1957 as *A Natu-ral Science of Society*).[27] In this seminar, Radcliffe–Brown was replying to professor Mortimer Adler's charge that the only possible social science was psychology.

Much like Durkheim before him, Radcliffe-Brown as-serted that each science deals with its own reality, with its own "natural system." When the elements of a system are unique to that system, and no other system in the universe, then a natural system can be said to exist and to form the basis for a distinctive science. "Social systems" are an emergent natural system that reveal unique properties that

[27]A. R. Radcliffe–Brown, *A Natural Science of Society* (New York: Free Press, 1948).

are not part of any other system in the universe. This property is *social relations* among individuals. Psychology, Radcliffe-Brown asserted, studies relations of properties within individuals, while sociology (and social anthropology) studies relations *between* individuals.

Thus, the task of the "natural science of society" is to discover the laws which govern the nature of social relations. Such discovery will be facilitated by the analysis of whole societies and by the comparison of findings about the operation of different types of societies. These, then, are the philosophical assumptions behind Radcliffe-Brown's functionalism. And as can be seen, he gave Durkheim's insistence that sociology study "social facts" and that society is an emergent reality, *sui generis,* new vigor for anthropologists.

RADCLIFFE-BROWN'S CONCEPTION OF SOCIAL STRUCTURE
For Radcliffe-Brown, the "natural science of society" examines social structures. Social structure "consists of the sum total of all social relationships of all individuals at a given moment in time. Although it cannot, naturally, be seen in its entirety at any one moment, we can observe it; all of the phenomenal reality is there."[28]

Thus, a science of society must explore the concrete patterns of social relations among individuals. For the societies studied by anthropologists, such relations are usually kinship relations, although any relatively enduring relation in a traditional society would be the topic of legitimate inquiry. It is for this reason that Radcliffe-Brown devoted much of his career to developing concepts which could describe kinship relations in primitive societies, and it is these concepts that the students and colleagues of Radcliffe-Brown were to use in their varied analyses of kinship systems. For in understanding kinship, much is known about social structure. And with comparative knowledge of social structures, laws of society can be formulated and tested.

An important point in Radcliffe-Brown's emphasis on structure is that it liberated anthropology from the global notions of culture as all the artifacts, beliefs, and customs of a people. We need only to recall Edward Tylor's definition

[28]Ibid., p. 55.

of culture as "that complex whole which includes knowledge, belief, art, morals, law, custom and any other capabilities and habits acquired by man as a member of society" to realize the significance of Radcliffe-Brown's emphasis on structure. This emphasis provided guidance for field researchers; it told them to focus on the actual patterns of relations among individuals. For field researchers overwhelmed in data, such advice often allowed them to see the "forest through the trees."

RADCLIFFE-BROWN'S COMMITMENT TO SYNCHRONIC ANALYSIS

We have noted how disillusioned Radcliffe-Brown became with evolutionary and historical methods as the analysis of a concrete society is undertaken. He proposed two distinctions for avoiding historical analysis of social structures. First, he distinguished "diachronic" from "synchronic" analysis. Diachronic inquiry involves the examination of social structures over time, while synchronic analysis is the observation of social structures at one point in time. Second, Radcliffe-Brown distinguished "ethnology" from "social anthropology." Ethnology was to be the study of a culture's history, while social anthropology was to formulate the general laws of social systems.[29]

This argument allowed field researchers to justify their activity. They could perform synchronic analysis and feel that they were true social scientists. Moreover, these distinctions put to rest, Radcliffe-Brown hoped, the last remnants of evolutionism and historicism.

RADCLIFFE-BROWN'S USE OF THE CONCEPTION OF FUNCTION

Radcliffe-Brown recognized that functional analysis is based upon an analogy between social and organic life. Yet curiously, he gave Durkheim most of the credit for this insight which, as we saw in the last chapter, more rightly belongs to Herbert Spencer. As Radcliffe-Brown remarked:[30] "The concept of function applied to human societies

---

[29]See, for example, his *Structure and Function in Primitive Societies* (London: Cohen & West, 1952) and *Method in Social Anthropology* (Chicago: University of Chicago Press, 1958).

[30]A. R. Radcliffe-Brown, "On the Concept of Function in Social Science," *American Anthropologist,* XXXVII (1935):394.

is based on an analogy between social life and organic life
.... So far as I know the first systematic formulation of the
concept as applying to the strictly scientific study of society
was that of Émile Durkheim."

Radcliffe-Brown went on to emphasize that functional
analysis consists of establishing "the correspondence between [a social institution] and the needs of the social organism."[31] He recognized, of course, the problems with such an
assertion: the dangers of an illegitimate teleology stemming
from assertions that the needs of the social organism cause
the emergence of the institution that meets these needs.[32]
To avoid this problem he suggested that the term "necessary conditions of existence" be substituted for "needs":[33]

> I would like to substitute for the term 'needs' the term 'neces-
> sary conditions of existence,' or, if the term 'need' is used, it
> is to be understood only in this sense. It may be noted, as a
> point to be returned to, that any attempt to apply this concept
> of function in social science involves the assumption that
> there *are* necessary conditions of existence for human soci-
> eties just as there are for animal organisms, and that they
> can be discovered by the proper kind of scientific enquiry.
> (emphasis in original)

Radcliffe-Brown often made analogies between social
and organic life, recognizing that "like all analogies it has
to be used with care." Yet, in his comparisons of social and
animal organisms, one is easily reminded of Spencer's early
efforts. One key distinction between social and organic life
is that in organic life "it is possible to observe the organic
structure to a large extent independently of its functioning.
It is therefore possible to make a morphology which is independent of physiology."[34] But in human societies "the social
structure as a whole can only be *observed* in its functioning" (emphasis in original). In other words social structures can only be seen and understood by reference to the
actual interactive processes in which individuals are en-

---

[31]Ibid.

[32]Yet, Radcliffe-Brown was often driven to utter extreme statements like: "Every custom and belief of a primitive society plays some determinate part in the
social life of the community, just as every organ of a living body plays some part
in the general life of an organism." *The Andaman Islanders,* op. cit., p. 229. Such
statements often led him back into the teleological trap that he wished to avoid.

[33]"On the Concept of Function," op. cit., p. 394.

[34]Ibid., p. 396.

gaged and which they use to form relatively enduring social relations, or social structure.

Thus, the concept of "functioning" refers to the processes of social life that go to create, maintain, and change social structure. The concept of "function" pertains to "the contribution which a partial activity makes to the total activity of which it is a part." Now, what determines "contribution"? Radcliffe-Brown's answer: the degree to which an activity meets the necessary conditions of existence of the social whole. And much like Durkheim before him, Radcliffe-Brown views the most critical "necessary conditions" to be social integration. In particular, he views two such conditions:[35] (1) the need for social systems to evidence "consistency" of structure, by which he meant: the establishment of clear rights and duties over things and persons so as to avoid conflict. (2) The need for social systems to reveal "continuity," by which he meant: the maintenance of rights and duties between persons so that interaction can proceed smoothly and regularly.

Much of Radcliffe-Brown's analysis of social activities and institutions in traditional societies was directed at showing how the activity or institution in question met one or both of these necessary conditions. For example, in his ethnography of the Andaman Islanders, he consistently analyzed social events in terms of the integrative needs, or necessary conditions, that they meet. In his analysis of ceremonies, for instance, Radcliffe-Brown often made the following kinds of statements:

> The purpose of the [peacemaking] ceremony is clearly to produce a change in the feelings of the two parties towards one another.[36]
>
> The essential character of all dancing is that it is rhythmical and it is fairly evident that the primary function of this rhythmical nature of the dance is to enable a number of persons to join in the same actions and perform them as one body.[37]
>
> The function of the dance-meetings was therefore to bring the two groups into contact and renew the social relations

[35] See, for a clear statement of this argument, his *Structure and Function in Primitive Society,* op. cit., p. 47.
[36] *Andaman Islanders,* op. cit., pp. 238–239.
[37] Ibid., p. 247.

between them and in that way to maintain the solidarity between them.[38]

[The painting of the body] is an action required by custom, the performance of which . . . serves to keep alive in the mind of the individual a certain system of sentiments necessary for the regulation in conformity to the needs of the society.[39]

Such analysis is, of course, reminiscent of Durkheim's examination of ritual in *Elementary Forms.* Radcliffe-Brown's later analysis of the functions of kinship was considerably more sophisticated in that he attempted to show how a particular kinship structure, such as a patrilineal descent system, operates to meet his two necessary conditions of existence.[40] It is Radcliffe-Brown's *structural analysis* of kinship which is impressive, since his *functional analysis* is, like Durkheim's, a foregone conclusion: the structure in question will meet his two conditions.

We might now ask: Why did Radcliffe-Brown employ the concept of function? What did it add to his description of the Andaman Islanders or his analyses of kinship structures? For Radcliffe-Brown, function was a concept that allowed him to avoid delving into the history of a people; it was a way to perform synchronic analysis and to believe that the discovery of functions could yield true laws of social systems:[41]

Any social system, to survive, must conform to certain conditions. If we can define adequately one of these universal conditions, i.e., one to which all human societies must conform, we have a sociological law. Thereupon if it can be shown that a particular institution in a particular society is the means by which that society conforms to the law, i.e., to the necessary condition, we may speak of this as the 'sociological origin' of the institution. Thus an institution may be said to have its general *raison d'être* (sociological origin) and its particular *raison d'être* (historical origin). The first is for the sociologist or social anthropologist to discover. . . . The second is for the historian. . . .

This statement summarizes the appeal of functional analysis and its problems. In essence, Radcliffe-Brown is

[38]Ibid., p. 253.
[39]Ibid., p. 275.
[40]See *Structure and Function,* op. cit., pp. 32–48.
[41]Ibid., p. 43.

asserting that if we can establish universal conditions of existence for social systems, we have a sociological law. And then, if we know the function of a structure for meeting these universal conditions, we have used our "law" to explain the existence (the "sociological origin") of this structure.

Radcliffe-Brown had thus fallen back into the trap that Durkheim wished to avoid in his distinction between cause and function. His commitment to synchronic analysis relegated the search for causes to the historian and made him, and many anthropologists and sociologists who followed him, feel that they had explained a social activity or social institution by asserting its function. Such a tactic made field work easier to interpret, since scientific explanation involved the "discovery" of the function of a structure in the social whole.

In sum, then, we can view Radcliffe-Brown's functionalism as rather simplistic and naive. He appears to have employed the concept of function as a way of forcing field researchers to focus on structures and as a way of avoiding discussions of evolution and historical origins. The power of Radcliffe-Brown's actual analyses of kinship structures should allow us to forgive his sloppy functional theorizing. Yet, his personal charisma set into motion many anthropological field workers who were committed to explanation by function.

Bronislaw Malinowski and the Preservation of Functionalism

Bronislaw Malinowski (1884–1942) extended functional analysis in wholly new directions. In contrast to Radcliffe-Brown, whose functionalism was confined to structural analysis of specific cultures, Malinowski developed an elaborate and abstract functional scheme which, on the one hand, was to repel many anthropologists while, on the other hand, to stimulate functional sociology. Had Malinowski not sought to elaborate functional analysis, it is unlikely that functionalism in sociology would have become the dominant paradigm in the late 1940s, 1950s, and early 1960s.

THE EVENTUAL REJECTION OF MALINOWSKI

Malinowski came to English anthropology after receiving his Ph.D. in physics and mathematics in Poland; in 1916 he received a social science degree in Britain. Early in his career (1915–1918) he conducted the classic ethnography on the Trobriand Islanders who lived off the coast of New Guinea. His ethnographic work, however, remained separated from his more abstract functional scheme.[42] Malinowski as the ethnographer remained unparalleled, but Malinowski as the functional theorist became embroiled in controversy and was eventually rejected and ignored in anthropology.

Part of this eventual rejection was due to the intellectual mood of the times. Radcliffe-Brown's and Boas's insistence on field work and upon theory inducted from concrete studies made Malinowski's a priori abstract scheme suspect. Moreover, as field researchers encountered problems in analyzing their data, Malinowski's grand scheme proved far less useful than Radcliffe-Brown's more concrete structural analysis.

Another part of Malinowski's rejection, however, stems from his personal intellectual style. While Radcliffe-Brown was the "gentleman-scholar," traveling the world over in the early decades of this century, Malinowski remained in England to fight for the recognition of functional thought. As the anthropologist, Meyer Fortes, notes of Malinowski:[43]

> One has to be able to visualize the histrionic, not to say the exhibitionist, streak in him to understand the tone of some of his later books. It arose from his view of himself as the leader of a revolutionary movement in anthropology.... He could not shake off the compulsion to present his theories... in the form of an assault upon the ancient regime.

Malinowski was commanding, dogmatic, and as some of his students argued, rather abrasive. Audrey Richards[44] said of

[42]Early in his career, Malinowski emphasized the importance of ethnographies, divorced of theory and speculation. As early as 1910 he wrote: " ... it is always good if the observer refrains from mixing his own theories with the related facts as much as possible." *Man* 10 (1910):139.

[43]"Malinowski and the Study of Kinship" in Raymond Firth's *Man and Culture: An Evaluation of the Work of Bronislaw Malinowski* (Chapel Hill: University of North Carolina Press, 1944) p. 157.

[44]Audrey I. Richards, "Bronislaw Kasper Malinowski," *Man* 33 (January–February, 1943):4.

him: "Pupils might be irritated by his intolerance, or enspired by his enthusiasms. They were never bored." Or, as another student suggested: "Invite Malinowski to the opening session of a conference. Half the audience will disagree with him violently, but the discussions will go with a swing from the start."[45] Or, as Raymond Firth put the matter: "He made unfriends as well as friends."[46]

Many who were irritated by Malinowski, we suspect, failed to appreciate his sardonic humor. For example, Malinowski's famous statement that "the magnificent title of the Functional School of Anthropology has been bestowed by myself, in a way on myself, and to a large extent out of my own sense of irresponsibility" is often cited as an indicator of his colossal arrogance. But in fact, he intended this statement as a joke—as a way of poking fun at those who sought to label schools of thought with individuals.

We have dwelled on Malinowski's personality for an important reason: Most of the analytical leads for the more elaborate functional schemes in sociology—especially that of the sociologist, Talcott Parsons—were present in Malinowski's work. In contrast, until very recently, anthropologists practiced Radcliffe-Brown's functionalism, ignoring and rejecting Malinowski's theoretical work. Sociologists, who had no vested interest in interpreting field data on primitives, and who were less involved in the personal and intellectual conflicts and antagonisms among anthropologists, found Malinowski's scheme appealing. Malinowski, the theorist, thus became the forgotten man in anthropology upon his death in 1942, while in sociology he was influencing the first generation of functional sociologists: Robert K. Merton, Kingsley Davis, Wilbert Moore, Marion Levy, and Talcott Parsons. This influence on sociology will be explored in the next chapter when we examine modern functionalism. Our task in this chapter is to understand Malinowski's abstract functional scheme.

MALINOWSKI'S OVERALL THEORETICAL STRATEGY
Malinowski, much like Radcliffe-Brown, was seeking an intellectual alternative to the extremes of evolutionism,

[45]Ibid.
[46]*Man and Culture: An Evaluation of the Work of Bronislaw Malinowski,* op. cit., p. 1.

diffusionism, and historical reconstruction. Functionalism for Malinowski offered a way of visualizing societies without reference to their past, while holding out the hope of generating the true laws of human organization.

How are these laws to be discovered? Malinowski stressed that a science of culture must be inductive; it must seek to ground itself in empirical facts: "Each scientific theory must start from a lead to observation." And yet, Malinowski appeared to have asked, how is it possible to order our observations of different cultures in a way that we can compare our observations and determine if they yield insight into the laws of culture? His answer was that a form of functional analysis could provide a common yardstick, or system of categories, for cataloguing and comparing observations.

The concept of function, therefore, was not as much an explanatory as a heuristic device. For he emphasized that "the concept of function is primarily descriptive."[47] The concept allows investigators to view the common features of cultures and to use their observations of what cultures have in common to generate social laws. As he noted:[48] "Sound generalization must be derived from comparison and the use of the inductive method, and here again, unless there is some theoretical common measure of comparison, our induction fails." For Malinowski, this "theoretical common measure of comparison" was to be found in the related concept of needs, institutions, and functions.

THE HIERARCHY OF NEEDS

Malinowski emphasized the importance of biological needs in shaping culture, for "man has, first and foremost, to satisfy all the needs of his organism."[49] Yet, once humans act to satisfy their biological needs, they create patterns of social organization and systems of symbols which embody new needs, or what Malinowski termed "derived needs":[50]

[47]Bronislaw Malinowski, *A Scientific Theory of Culture and Other Essays* (Chapel Hill: University of North Carolina Press, 1944), p. 116.
[48]Bronislaw Malinowski, "Man's Culture and Man's Behavior," *American Scientist* 29 (October, 1941):198.
[49]Malinowski, *A Scientific Theory,* op. cit., p. 37.
[50]Malinowski, "Man's Culture and Man's Behavior," op. cit., p. 201.

It is obvious, however, that culture solves not merely simple organic problems, but creates new problems, inspires new desires, and establishes a new universe in which man moves, never completely free from his organic needs, but also following new needs and stimulated by new satisfactions.

Thus, contrary to his many critics, Malinowski was never seeking to explain cultural patterns in terms of biological needs. He merely emphasized that such needs placed broad constraints, or limits, on the forms of cultural elaboration that are possible. But he leaves little doubt that it is the emergent cultural structures and systems of symbols that constitute the main body of anthropological investigation. Indeed, as he asserted, "the less directly organic the need to which human behavior refers, the more likely it will breed those phenomena which have provided the greatest amount of food for anthropological speculation."[51]

Malinowski's schemes involved an effort to classify the types of needs existing at three different levels: the biological, the social structural, and the symbolic. Anthropology should, he emphasized, concentrate on the ways in which social structural and symbolic needs are met, for these will not only provide "food for anthropological speculation," but also the necessary heuristic device, or comparative yardstick, for organizing data on human cultures. We can best visualize this emphasis by briefly reviewing Malinowski's discussion of biological, social structural, and symbolic needs.

Biological Needs   At various places, Malinowski refers to biological needs as "primary" needs—a label which could lead to misinterpretation, since "primary" can connote "most important." But what Malinowski sought to do was list the basic biological needs of the individual human organism and then show how these needs necessitate action for their fulfillment. Such action becomes collectively organized and symbolically integrated, but these cultural responses must incorporate certain "vital sequences" that are tied to the facts of human biology. In Table 1, Malinowski's list of biological needs and the necessary biological acts for their satisfaction are listed. For Malinowski, this list must

[51]*A Scientific Theory,* op. cit., p. 73.

TABLE 1 Permanent Vital Sequences Incorporated in All Cultures

(A) Impulse →	(B) Act →	(C) Satisfaction
Drive to breathe; gasping for air	intake of oxygen	elimination of CO_2 in tissues
hunger	ingestion of food	satiation
thirst	absorption of liquid	quenching
sex appetite	conjugation	detumescence
fatigue	rest	restoration of muscular and nervous energy
restlessness	activity	satisfaction of fatigue
somnolence	sleep	awakening with restored energy
bladder pressure	micturition	removal of tension
colon pressure	defecation	abdominal relaxation
fright	escape from danger	relaxation
pain	avoidance by effective act	return to normal state

be incorporated into human culture, lest individuals die. But the key point is that in incorporating these vital sequences, humans elaborate social structure and cultural symbols—thereby creating new or derived needs. If the most basic of these derived needs are not met, then culture, like the individual, also "dies" or ceases to exist.

Social Structural or "Instrumental Needs" As humans become organized to meet biological needs, they create "social institutions." The concept of institutions is central to Malinowski's view of culture, since it is the major structural category of his analysis. Institutions, for Malinowski, are organized activities among humans revealing a definite structure. And institutional analysis is the key to anthropological inquiry:[52]

> No element, trait, custom, or idea is defined or can be defined except by placing it within its relevant and real institutional setting. We are thus insisting that such institutional analysis is not only possible but indispensable. It is maintained here that the institution is the real isolate of cultural analysis.

For Malinowski, all institutions reveal certain common elements. Each has a "personnel"—that is, people. Each has a "charter" or defined reasons, purposes, and goals for its

[52]Ibid., p. 54.

members' participation. Each has a set of "norms," or rules about how personnel are to behave. Each has typical "activities" that its members are to perform. Each reveals a "material apparatus" or implements such as tools or facilities such as buildings for the conduct of activity. And each institution has a function—that is, it meets some need of its members or of the culture as a whole.

Malinowski then sought to demonstrate that there are certain universal institutions found in all cultures. For "although institutions such as the family, state, age-group, or religious congregation vary as between one culture and another, and in some cases, within the same culture, it is possible to draw up a list of types or classes representative of any and every culture."[53] One of his lists is presented in Table 2.

Why did Malinowski construct such a list? He would probably have answered that it is essential for field workers to have a procedure for classifying cultures. If a comprehensive list of universal institutions can guide field workers in their observations, then each investigation will have a common "check list" for describing a culture's institutions. In this way, descriptions of cultures will be comparable, and variations between cultures can be compared in regard to how their institutions are organized. And if institutional structures can be compared with the same conceptual yardstick, then perhaps the laws of institutional organization can be uncovered.

Malinowski viewed institutions as instrumental—as accomplishing something for humans. This is explicit in his notion that along with the elements of personnel, charter, norms, activities, and material apparatus, each institution has a function. At one level institutions incorporate the "vital sequences" necessary for survival of the human organism. But once people organize their biological sequences into institutions, new needs emerge. These are the needs that must be met if collective organization of humans is to be possible. Thus, once humans create social structures, or institutions, these emergent structures have imperatives or needs, as vital and real as those of the individual organism, that must be met if the "social organism" is to survive.

[53]Ibid., p. 55.

TABLE 2   List of Universal Institutional Types

Major Focus	Types of Institution
1. Reproduction (*Bonds of blood defined by a legal contract of marriage and extended by a specifically defined principle of descent on the genealogical scheme.*)	The family, as the domestic group of parents and children. Courtship organization. The legal definition and organization of marriage as a contract binding two individuals and relating two groups. The extended domestic group and its legal, economic, and religious organization. Groups of kindred united on the unilateral principle of descent. The clan, matrilineal or patrilineal. The system of related clans.
2. Territorial (*Community of interests due to propinquity, contiguity, and possibility of cooperation.*)	The neighborhood group of municipalities, such as the nomadic horde, the roaming local band, the village, the cluster of hamlets or homesteads, the town, the city. The district, the province, the tribe (Cf. 7).
3. Physiological (*Distinctions due to sex, age, and bodily stigmata or symptoms.*)	Primitive sex totemic groups. Organizations based on physiological or anatomical sex distinctions. Organizations due to sexual division of functions and activities. Age groups and age-grades, insofar as they are organized. Organizations in primitive societies of the abnormal, the mentally deranged, the epileptics (often connected with magical or religious ideas); at higher levels, institutions for the sick, the insane, the congenitally defective.
4. Voluntary Associations	Primitive secret societies, clubs, recreational teams, artistic societies. At higher levels, the clubs, mutual aid and benefit societies, lodges, voluntary associations for recreation, uplift, or the realization of a common purpose.
5. Occupational and Professional (*The organization of human beings by their specialized activities for the purpose of common interest and a fuller achievement of their special abilities.*)	At a primitive level, primarily of magicians, sorcerers, shamans, and priests; also guilds of craftsmen and economic teams. As civilization develops, the innumerable workshops, guilds, and undertakings, economic interest groups, and associations of professional workers in medicine, in law, in teaching, and in ministering to religious needs.

(Table 2 continues)

51

TABLE 2   (Continued)

Major Focus	Types of Institution
	Also specific units for the organized exercise of teaching (schools, colleges, universities); for research (laboratories, academies, institutes); for administration of justice (legislative bodies, courts, police force); for defence and aggression (army, navy, air force); for religion (parish, sects, churches).
6. Rank and Status	Estates and orders of nobility, clergy, burghers, peasants, serfs, slaves. The caste system.
	Stratification by ethnic, that is, either racial or cultural distinctions at primitive and developed levels.
7. Comprehensive (*The integration by community of culture or by political power.*)	The tribe as the cultural unit corresponding to nationality at more highly developed levels.
	The cultural sub-group in the regional sense or in the sense of small enclaves (alien minorities, the ghetto, the gypsies).
	The political unit which may comprise part of the tribe or its totality or yet include several cultural subdivisions. The distinction between tribe-nation and tribe-state as a political organization is fundamental.

Unlike Radcliffe-Brown or Durkheim, however, Malinowski was not content to assert a need for integration, and then routinely analyze institutions with respect to how they function to maintain integration. In contrast, Malinowski developed a list of four basic "instrumental needs" for collective patterns of social organization. These are presented in Table 3.

Each social institution, to remain a viable structure, must meet these four needs, or requisites. Moreover, the social structure of a culture as a whole—that is, the congerie of all its institutions—must also be viewed as having to meet these needs. This fact creates a situation where institutions tend to specialize or have functions for meeting one instrumental need more than the other three. For example, the institutions of "tribe" and "cultural subgroup" listed at the bottom of Table 1 meet the political organization needs of

TABLE 3   Malinowski's Instrumental Needs

1. The cultural apparatus of implements and consumers' goods must be produced, used, maintained, and replaced by new production.
    Economics
	2. Human behavior, as regards its technical, customary, legal, or moral prescription must be codified, regulated in action and sanctioned.
	    Social control

3. The human material by which every institution is maintained must be renewed, formed, drilled, and provided with full knowledge of tribal tradition.
    Education
	4. Authority within each institution must be defined, equipped with powers, and endowed with means of forceful execution of its orders.
	    Political organization

This table appears exactly as it did in his work. We note here the similarity of these needs and their mode of presentation to those that are later to be developed by Talcott Parsons.

a culture more than the economic or education needs. Yet, even with this kind of "specialization," each institution as an entity must meet all four instrumental imperatives to survive as a social structure, while meeting all four needs of the broader cultural whole if the cultural whole is to be maintained.

In sum, then, Malinowski's list of universal institutions was intended to aid in comparative analysis of ethnographic data. By analyzing the elements of each institution —its personnel, its charter, its norms, its activities, its material apparatus, and its function (whether economic, educational, political, or social control)—anthropology would have a heuristic device for true comparative analysis. By describing (a) who is involved in an institution (that is, its personnel); (b) what its purpose is (that is, its charter); (c) what its key norms are (the normative element); (d) what the nature of its tools and facilities are (the material apparatus); (e) what the nature and division of activities are (the element of activity); (f) which instrumental need(s) are most involved (the element of function); anthropological descriptions would provide a common content for those wishing to use this content to generalize and to discover the laws of cultural organization.

Symbolic or Integrative Needs   As humans have sought to organize collectively to deal with biological and instrumental needs, they have also created symbol systems. They have generated in the course of their activities systems of ideas that they use to legitimate, regulate, and guide their conduct. Symbols are thus used to integrate, to weld together institutions and complexes of institutions into a unified and coherent whole.

Malinowski was much less comprehensive and clear in his analysis of integrative needs. Basically he appears to have urged that the creation and use of symbols establishes new imperatives. He isolates three basic types of these derived integrative needs:[54] (1) the need for members of a society to have, use, and transmit a system of principles for dealing with the world around them. He considered the "knowledge" of a culture to be the system of symbols meeting this need. (2) The need for the members of a society to have a sense that they control their destiny and chance events in the world around them. Malinowski viewed magic and religion as the principal symbol systems meeting this need. And (3), the need for members of a society to share a "communal rhythm" in their activities and lives. Malinowski saw this need as being met by those systems of thought guiding art, sports, games, and ceremonies.

The isolation of distinctive types of thought systems that meet each of these three integrative needs was viewed by Malinowski as yet another tool for comparative analysis. All cultures, he asserted, will reveal coherent symbol systems, and if we can isolate the basic types of such systems, just as is proposed for social institutions, then we have another heuristic device for recording and comparing variations among cultures. Thus, in essence, Malinowski stressed that while institutional analysis was perhaps the most central, an understanding of a culture required observations on the knowledge, magic, religious, artistic, sports, and ceremonial symbols employed by a people as they carry out their institutional activities.

MALINOWSKI'S FUNCTIONAL SCHEME:
A RETROSPECTIVE ASSESSMENT
Malinowski once uttered in an article written for a lay audience:[55] "The functional view of culture insists therefore

---

[54]Bronislaw Malinowski, "The Group and the Individual in Functional Analysis," *American Journal of Sociology,* XLIV (6, 1939):938–964.

[55]Bronislaw Malinowski, "Anthropology," *Encyclopedia Britannica,* 1st supplementary vol. (New York, 1936):132.

upon the principle that in every type of civilization, every custom, material object, idea and belief fulfills some vital function." This is, of course, an incredible statement and it has often been used to dismiss Malinowski's functional scheme.[56] It would seem to state that all cultural items meet needs, or they would not exist in a culture. Moreover, it is a short analytical step to asserting that the existence of an item is caused by the need it serves.

But we should look deeper into Malinowski's intended meaning. One matter to consider is the intellectual traditions against which Malinowski was reacting. He was, along with Radcliffe-Brown, attempting to discredit evolutionism. This tradition often viewed cultural items as dead "survivals" of past evolutionary stages or as historical products whose origin must be discerned. Moreover, Malinowski was also attacking the extreme diffusionism of his day which argued that cultural traits were borrowed. Thus, at one level, Malinowski's statement can be seen as a polemic against efforts to view cultural items as evolutionary holdovers, historical byproducts, and disconnected traits. As a polemic, his statement would be extreme and would stress that cultural items exist because they work—that is, they facilitated adaptation in the past and they meet humans' biological, organizational, and symbolic needs in the present. Therefore, as he always stressed, we must examine cultural items in terms of their consequences for the living culture of today. They are not "idle survivals or disconnected traits, but they function—that is, they are at work."[57]

Another reason behind Malinowski's extreme statements is his horror at what "civilized" peoples were doing to traditional societies. He observed the efforts of traders, missionaries, and colonial governments to impose "civilization" on a people, thereby disrupting their way of life. As he noted:[58]

Everywhere the same fanatical zeal to prune, uproot, make *auto-da-fe* of all that shocks our own moral, hygenic or parochial susceptibilities, the same ignorant and stupid lack of

[56]*See,* for example, Jonathan H. Turner, *The Structure of Sociological Theory,* op. cit. and Robert K. Merton, "Manifest and Latent Functions" in his *Social Theory and Social Structure* (Glencoe, Ill.: The Free Press, 1949).

[57]Bronislaw Malinowski, "Culture as a Determinant of Behavior," *Human Affairs* edited by R. B. Cattell (New York: Macmillan, 1937), p. 179.

[58]Bronislaw Malinowski, "Ethnology and the Study of Society," *Economica* 2 (6, 1921):214.

comprehension of the fact that every item of culture, every custom and belief, represents a value, fulfills a social function. . . .

Our damning quote thus takes on new meaning. It represents an early (1921) plea for people to recognize that one cannot change traits of a culture without disrupting the cultural whole, without disrupting the essence and being of a people.

In these two contexts—one intellectual and the other moral outrage—many of Malinowski's extreme statements can be forgiven. But anthropologists were not to forgive or overlook, leaving it to sociologists to become intrigued with Malinowski's scheme.

If we compare Durkheim's and Radcliffe-Brown's functionalism with Malinowski's, we can perhaps appreciate Malinowski's appeal to early sociologists. Durkheim and Radcliffe-Brown asserted essentially one need of social structure—the need for integration—and then proceeded to analyze how a given structure, whether the division of labor, religious ritual, or a kinship pattern, met this need for integration. Such an approach is as simple as it is mundane to sociologists seeking to understand complex, modern societies. Imagine, for example, how fruitless it would seem to describe in detail the properties of such modern structures as bureaucracy, urban communities, the political state, and the mass educational system, only to end with the conclusion that these "function" to meet integrative needs.

Malinowski's scheme was more complex and thus provided more analytical options. Social structures could be distinguished in terms of *which* needs they met. Moreover, social structural needs were distinguished from symbolic needs, allowing sociologists to separate structural analysis of institutions from the analysis of idea systems. Indeed, the notion of system levels—the biological, psychological, the social, and cultural (symbols)—was given forceful expression by Malinowski. Each system level must be examined separately in terms of its own needs or requirements for survival, and yet, the interdependence of systems in the "web of life" must also be understood. Thus, Malinowski presented sociological functionalism with many of its key points of emphasis:

1. Social reality exists at different levels, minimally the biological, psychological, social, and cultural (symbolic).
2. The properties of these levels must be understood by separate sciences, but the interconnectedness of levels forces the analyst of the social or institutional level to recognize how biological, psychological, and cultural (symbolic) needs impinge upon social structural arrangements.
3. Systems can be analyzed in terms of their needs. Parts in a system exist because they have had selective advantage over other parts in meeting needs. Analysts are therefore justified in seeking to understand the relation of a part to systemic needs.
4. At the social system level, the needs for economic adaptation, political control, legal and moral integration, and educational socialization are important in understanding the place and operation of institutions in social systems.

This was Malinowski's legacy which, partly because of his personality and extreme polemics, was to be rejected in anthropological theorizing. And yet, it was to stimulate the sociological imagination, creating a functional orientation which, until recently, dominated sociology. It is to modern sociological and anthropological functionalism that we now direct our attention.

3

Modern Functionalism in Anthropology and Sociology

In the 1930s, the presence of Radcliffe-Brown and Malinowski in American universities began to influence not only anthropological theory, but also conceptual work in sociology. Functional theory in anthropology, however, did not develop much beyond Malinowski's formulations. Functionalism as a method and approach for gathering and interpreting data on specific societies continued to prosper, and even later efforts to revise and revive functionalism emphasized its utility as a method. In anthropology, then, functionalism was to remain a method for collecting and organizing data in a way that would allow for the laws of human organization to be inducted.

It was in sociology that Malinowski's insights, coupled with the rediscovery of Durkheim's work, were to exert enormous influence in the development of functionalism as a *theoretical* approach to understanding the social world. Early sociology did not have a large body of data which required interpretation, and thus, the adoption of the functional orientation remained unencumbered by the need to use functionalism as a method for data displays. Rather, Malinowski's lead could inspire the elaboration of abstract conceptual schemes which were not tied to a vast body of ethnographic data.

Early Functional Schemes in Sociology

THE DAVIS-MOORE HYPOTHESIS

In 1945 the first major functional theory in sociology was published. Kingsley Davis and Wilbert Moore presented a theory of stratification in which notions of survival needs or functional requisites were central.[1] The Davis and Moore hypothesis, as their theory became known, concerned the issue of how and why social positions within a society receive unequal shares of scarce and valuable resources, such as money, prestige, honor, and power. They entitled their theory "Some Principles of Stratification," but in point of fact they enumerated only one major principle that we have taken the liberty of formalizing in the following manner: "The more functionally important positions in a system, and the less available qualified personnel to fill these positions, the greater the inducements necessary to attract qualified personnel, and hence, the greater the rewards attached to these positions."

This principle summarizes a more elaborate argument that can be presented as follows:

1. All societies have certain survival requisites which must be met. They require, for example, technical knowledge, government, and religious symbols (Davis and Moore do not provide an exhaustive list of basic requisites).[2]

2. Certain positions in a social system are more central to meeting these requisites than others.

3. If a society is to survive, it must somehow assure that all functionally important positions—that is, those central to meeting survival requisites—are filled with qualified personnel.

4. Rewards are allocated in a society in proportion to the relative difficulty of securing personnel to fill these functionally important positions. However, if a position is functionally important and easy to fill,

---

[1] Kingsley Davis and Wilbert E. Moore, "Some Principles of Stratification," *American Sociological Review*, 10 (April, 1945):242–247.

[2] Davis was one of several authors to propose such a list several years later. *See*, in particular, D. F. Aberle, A. K. Cohen, A. K. Davis, M. J. Levy, F. Y. Sutton, "The Functional Requisites of a Society," *Ethics*, LX (January, 1950):100–111 and Kingsley Davis, *Human Society* (New York: Macmillan, 1948).

then it will not receive high rewards. It is only when a position is functionally important *and* difficult to fill that it will receive high rewards.

5. Most positions that are difficult to fill require an unusual amount of training or talent.

6. Thus, the differential allocation of rewards is a mechanism by which actors are induced to use their talents in, or undergo the training necessary for participation in, these functionally important positions.

7. Therefore, stratification or the unequal distribution of rights and privileges, or rewards, is a mechanism that has evolved in social systems to assure that functionally important positions are filled with qualified personnel.

This hypothesis set off a debate and controversy that persists to the present day,[3] but our purposes are not served by reviewing the many criticisms of the Davis-Moore hypothesis. Rather, we should emphasize the significance of this argument for the subsequent development of functional theory in sociology.

Probably the most significant aspect of the Davis-Moore hypothesis is the central place of functional requisites as *explanatory* concepts. Unlike Malinowski, where needs and requisites were considered useful only as a heuristic and descriptive device, the Davis-Moore hypothesis uses functional needs in a new way, since they are now transformed into a key independent variable in a theory of stratification.

THE GROWING CONCERN OVER FUNCTIONAL REQUISITES

At the time Davis and Moore were formulating their theory, other social scientists became intrigued with cataloguing the needs and requisites of society. While their published efforts did not appear until the early 1950s, various groups of Harvard students and faculty had begun to construct lists of functional prerequisites. For example, a joint statement by David Aberle, Albert Cohen, Kingsley Davis, Marion Levy, and Francis Sutton marked the culmination of one

---

[3]*See,* for example, Melvin M. Tumin, "Some Principles of Stratification: A Critical Analysis," *American Sociological Review,* 18 (April, 1953):387–394.

Harvard seminar.[4] These authors began with a statement of the four conditions that would cause the termination of society: (1) the biological extinction of its members, (2) the apathy of its members, (3) a war of all against all, and (4) the absorption of the society into another. (We might note that (1), (2), and (3) were similar to three of Malinowski's "derived needs" of social structure.) These four conditions offered a criterion for assessing functions: If the absence of a function would result in any four of these conditions causing societal termination, then it could be considered a functional prerequisite of society. The authors then constructed a list of what must be done—that is, a list of requisites—if a society is to survive: (a) provision for adequate relationship to the environment and for sexual recruitment, (b) role differentiation and assignment, (c) communication, (d) shared cognitive orientations, (e) shared, articulated set of goals, (f) the normative regulation of means, (g) the regulation of affective expression, and (h) socialization. In this list can be found Malinowski's instrumental and integrative needs as well as the needs of the functional requisite system to be developed subsequently by Talcott Parsons who was, of course, an instructor of all these authors. There was, no doubt, considerable mutual inspiration between Parsons and these Harvard protégées.

While the Davis-Moore hypothesis and the adoption of functional requisite analysis stood at the forefront of the functional movement in sociology, these efforts were but surface manifestations stirred earlier by another Harvard fellow, Robert K. Merton. Merton, who was to present his own functional approach in 1949, taught a course while a graduate student at Harvard.[5] Both Kingsley Davis and Wilbert Moore were also graduate students at Harvard, although not exact contemporaries. Moore, in particular, was exposed to Merton's discussions of Radcliffe-Brown and Malinowski, as were several of the authors who developed lists of functional requisites; and when Moore and Davis became colleagues at Pennsylvania State University, Mer-

---

[4]Aberle, et al., op. cit.
[5]Thanks to Wilbert E. Moore for informing us of this course and of Merton's influence on his fellow students.

ton's influence apparently shaped their analysis of stratification.

Thus, the major figure in functional sociology during the late 1930s and early 1940s was Robert K. Merton. Only much later in the early 1950s was the elaborate Parsonian scheme to unfold, although Parsons recognized in the mid-1940s that functional theory was to provide sociology with a coherent conceptual framework.[6] Other important functional works by members of this Harvard group, such as Marion J. Levy's *The Structure of Society*[7] and Kingsley Davis' *Human Societies,*[8] were also produced from the intellectual milieu provided by Merton's and Parsons' concern with functionalism.

It is clear, then, that by the 1940s, sociologists had become intrigued with what Malinowski had termed "derived needs." Sociological functionalism was thus to elaborate the notion of survival requisites and it was to make them central to the development of conceptual schemes in sociology.

There was, however, an early warning as to the dangers of this line of theoretical development by the very person who had informally brought Radcliffe-Brown and Malinowski into the Harvard sociological circle, Robert K. Merton. Thus, before examining the elaboration of functional theory in sociology and the functional method in anthropology, we should pause briefly to examine Merton's warning and the functional protocol that his reservations led him to advocate.

Robert K. Merton's Functional Protocol

In the 1949 edition of his classic, *Social Theory and Social Structure,*[9] Merton notes that "functional analysis is at once the most promising and least codified of contemporary orientations." Merton emphasizes that functionalism rep-

[6]Talcott Parsons, "The Present Position and Prospects of Systematic Theory in Sociology," *Essays in Sociological Theory* (New York: Free Press, 1949).

[7]Marion J. Levy, Jr., *The Structure of Society* (Princeton, N.J.: Princeton University Press, 1952).

[8]Op. cit.

[9]Robert K. Merton, "Manifest and Latent Functions," *Social Theory and Social Structure* (New York: Free Press, 1968, originally published in the 1949 edition; all references here pertain to the 1968 edition).

resents a "triple alliance between theory, method, and data." That is, functionalism, on the one hand, is a useful method for collecting and arranging data, while on the other hand, it promises to be a useful way to interpret and explain regularities that emerge from empirical investigations. Merton views, incorrectly we suspect, the methodological component of functionalism to be the weakest. Yet, as the eloquent advocate of the "middle range" strategy for theory building, he recognizes that functional methods should lead to data collection and arrangement that facilitates functional theorizing, or functional interpretations of data.

Thus Merton's analysis of functionalism is directed toward creating an approach that guides both data collection and its theoretical interpretation. As we seek to understand Merton's functional scheme, then, we must recognize that it represents not so much a conceptual scheme as a way of facilitating the interchange between empirical investigations and theoretical activity.

QUESTIONABLE POSTULATES IN FUNCTIONAL ANALYSIS

Merton devotes considerable effort to questioning three "functional postulates" that he feels have come to dominate functional inquiry: (1) the postulate of "functional unity," (2) the postulate of "universal functionalism," and (3) the postulate of "indispensability." He accuses both Malinowski and Radcliffe-Brown of implicitly employing these postulates in their work, and hence, his analysis of these postulates represents an effort to correct for the deficiencies of anthropological functionalism.

The "functional unity" postulate holds that social systems *must* reveal high degrees of integration among their constituent parts. Such an assumption, Merton stresses, can allow investigators to simply assume unity and then mechanically view social structures as contributing to this unity or integration. Merton argues that the degree of integration in a system is always an empirical question and should be the end product, not an a priori assumption, of careful empirical investigation. For only through investigation of particular empirical systems can the level, degree, and nature of integration be determined.

The "functional universality" postulate holds that if a

structure exists in an ongoing social system, then it must have positive functions for the maintenance of this system. Merton emphasizes that such an assumption often results in tautologous arguments: Item A exists in system S; system S exists and persists; therefore, item A must promote the persistence of system S. Merton quotes Malinowski's famous overstatement that "every custom, material object, idea and belief fulfills some vital function" as evidence of this tendency of anthropological functionalists to employ the "functional universality" postulate, but as we noted in the last chapter, there were both intellectual and moral reasons for Malinowski's extreme assertion. Moreover, Malinowski argued this way only in popular, lay-oriented publications, not in his more scholarly and conceptual works. Yet it must be acknowledged that this postulate often implicitly guided, and still guides today, much anthropological inquiry. If an item exists in a culture, it must "do something" for its survival, otherwise it would not be there.

What Merton wishes to stress in calling attention to this implicit postulate is that the functions of an item—that is, its consequences for a system—are an empirical question and must be determined only after careful examination of the part in relationship to system members, other system parts, and the systemic whole. For indeed, an item may have varied consequences—positive, negative, and non-functional—for different system referents. To assume that a part has "positive functions" is to define away all the interesting empirical questions.

The "postulate of indispensability" holds that systems have functional requisites or needs that must be met if they are to survive, and therefore, system parts must operate to meet these needs. A corollary to this postulate is that only certain types of structures can meet certain system requisites. Again, Merton stresses that the functional requisites —that is, what a system needs to do in order to survive— must be empirically established for *each* system under study. Requisites will vary, Merton argues, for different empirical systems existing in widely varying environments. Moreover, the easily documented fact that many alternative parts can evolve in a system to meet similar requisites throws into doubt the corollary that only certain parts can meet particular functional requisites. The key questions for functional analysis, Merton stresses, must therefore be on establishing the requisites for a system under study and then assessing the range and variety of structural adaptations that can evolve to meet these requisites.

Merton's critique of these three postulates represents a concerted effort on his part to avoid some of the dangers of functional analysis. Malinowski and Radcliffe-Brown often employed these postulates, as did many other field ethnographers, although we suspect that Merton has overemphasized the extent to which these postulates distorted anthropological theorizing and data collection. Yet, they highlight certain inherent problems in functionalism and allow Merton to stress the importance of:[10] (a) viewing social systems as empirical facts, not abstract and reified analytical systems; (b) establishing for each empirical system the consequences—whether functional, dysfunctional, or nonfunctional—of specific parts for different system referents; and (c) assessing the degree to which specific parts and processes within the system meet empirically established survival requisites or needs. In this way, functionalism can guide rather than hinder empirical investigation of social systems.

This concern with assuring that theory is connected to data collection, and that data collection has theoretical significance, leads Merton to develop a "paradigm" of functional analysis. In reality this "paradigm" is more of a research and theory building protocol. It is not theory in that it does not develop abstract concepts or propositions. Rather, it is a set of instructions, as well as a series of warnings, about how to conduct functional data collection and how to build functional interpretations of data.

MERTON'S "PARADIGM" OF FUNCTIONAL ANALYSIS

We cannot communicate the subtlety and depth of Merton's protocol here, only its broad contours.[11] The first step in his protocol is description of the phenomenon of interest to an investigator, for only through description can the nature of the context in which certain structures operate be exposed.

[10]Jonathan H. Turner, *The Structure of Sociological Theory* (Homewood, Ill.: The Dorsey Press, 1974), p. 65.

[11]*See* pp. 104–109 in *Social Theory and Social Structure,* op. cit., for details of the paradigm.

A second necessary procedure is to describe the "meaning" of a situation for the actors implicated in process and structures of interest to an investigator. Understanding the significance of events to actors can often offer clues as to the reasons behind, or "manifest functions" of, certain events. A related step is to determine the motives for both deviation and conformity among participants in processes and structures of concern to an investigator. In this way, clues about the psychological needs being served by particular facets of a system can be uncovered. However, to focus on the conscious states of actors can skew analysis away from consequences of structures and processes that are unintended and unrecognized by participants. Thus, investigators must be attuned not just to manifest, but also to "latent functions" of events.

These initial concerns allow for a more adequate assessment of the function served by particular system parts. The emphasis is on description of (1) a part, (2) the social context in which it is imbedded, and (3) the psychological states of actors. In this way, the analyst is alerted to different system referents—individuals, other structures, and systemic wholes—for which a particular part can have functions. The concern with "manifest" and "latent" functions attunes the investigator to the fact that functional consequences can be intended and unintended, as well as recognized and not recognized.

The next step in the functional analysis of an empirical system concerns the assessment of requisites that exist for various system referents: individuals, subparts, and the systemic whole. Now, it is possible to assess the "net balance of consequences" of an item. This assessment involves determining if an item of concern has positive (functional), negative (dysfunctional), or no discernible consequences for various system referents. Such assessment is assisted by understanding the requisites of various system referents and by concern with objective consequences, whether manifest or latent, of an item. Functional analysis thus becomes a kind of "balance sheet" of functions and dysfunctions for different aspects of a system.

The assessment of the balance of functions must include additional steps. One involves isolation of the "mechanisms" through which an item has its various consequences on a system. What are the *specific* social processes by which functions are exerted? Another step concerns the question as to whether or not alternative structures, operating through alternative mechanisms, could have the same functions. In this way, speculation about the range of potential variations of substructures in systems is possible. And a final crucial step involves assessing the degree to which the balance of functions promotes or retards social change and stability.

What Merton proposes, therefore, is a way to conduct functional analysis without implicitly employing the questionable postulates of "functional unity," "functional indispensability," and "functional universality." Merton's protocol has, as have all functional approaches, been subject to criticism.[12] Our intent here, however, is only to emphasize that the first systematic presentation of a functional approach in sociology was decidedly empirical in emphasis and was concerned primarily with developing a *method* of inquiry rather than an abstract conceptual scheme. In this sense, Merton's work is in the anthropological camp, since it emphasizes functional theory that is tied to empirical facts, and to bodies of descriptive data.

But as the Davis-Moore hypothesis foreshadowed, sociological theorizing is often more abstract, seeking to explain all social systems. Thus, the Davis-Moore hypothesis sought to explain all stratification systems, not just the operation and functioning of stratification in a particular society. Indeed, sociological theorizing, in the tradition of its first European masters,[13] has often sought to do more: to explain the structure and dynamics of large scale systems, such as societies or systems of societies.

Functionalism offered a way to understand all social processes. The notion of functional requisites was to provide the key that held out this promise. If the universal requisites of all social systems can be established, then it is possible to understand the dynamics of systems in terms of how structures evolve and operate to meet these requisites. This line of argument represents a subtle, and yet radical, departure from Malinowski's and Merton's view that the concept

---

[12]*See* Turner, op. cit., pp. 71–73.
[13]*See* Lewis A. Coser's *Masters of Sociological Thought,* second edition, New York: Harcourt, Brace, Jovanovich, 1977 for the best analysis of these masters.

of function is a heuristic device or method for approaching data collection and analysis. As we noted in the Davis-Moore hypothesis, function is now an *explanatory principle* which is to encourage the development of elaborate and abstract schemes about social systems *in general.* [14] Gone is the concern with specific empirical systems. In its place is an emphasis on abstract social systems and on the principles governing their functioning. Merton[15] argues eloquently against this change in emphasis, asserting that "a total system of sociological theory, in which observations about every aspect of social behavior, organization, and change promptly find their preordained place, has the same exhilarating challenge and the same small promise as those many all-encompassing philosophical systems which have fallen into deserved disuse." Whether Merton's warning is correct can still be considered a matter of debate, but it is clear that during the 1950s and 1960s, Malinowski's earlier cataloguing of universal requisites and needs of different system levels—the biological, social structural, and symbolic—was to stimulate the development of elaborate functional schemes. The most elaborate and influential of these schemes is that developed by Talcott Parsons.

Abstract Functional Schemes: Talcott Parsons' "Action Theory"

PARSONS' EARLY THEORY OF ACTION

Talcott Parsons' early work does not foretell of the elaborate theoretical system that he was to develop. His first work,[16] *The Structure of Social Action,* was published in 1937—at about the time that Malinowski's scheme had become fully developed. This work, however, reveals few hints of the functional analysis to follow. It is concerned primarily with synthesizing diverse lines of thought into a conception of

[14]Less obvious reliance on requisites as an explanatory principle can be found in Davis', op. cit., and Levy's, op. cit., analyses of human societies. These two books, after close to three decades, are still the two best descriptions of the structure and dynamics of societal systems. For a more recent effort that is in this tradition, *see:* Jonathan H. Turner, *Patterns of Social Organization* (New York: McGraw-Hill, 1972).

[15]*Social Theory,* op. cit., p. 45.

[16]Talcott Parsons, *The Structure of Social Action* (New York: McGraw-Hill, 1937).

action as (1) goal directed; (2) as involving the selection of appropriate means among alternatives; (3) as being regulated by ideas; and (4) as being circumscribed by physical-biological parameters.

Parsons in this early phase is thus concerned with the basic "elements" that are involved in human action. And in many ways, it is an analysis of individual action not collective action among corporate units such as groups and organizations. Diagrammatically, Parsons' early scheme can be represented as in Figure 3.1.

Yet, while there is no mention of functions and system needs in *The Structure of Social Action,* two concerns appear to have dictated the eventual development of a functional orientation. One of these concerns is Parsons' tendency, inherited from Max Weber,[17] to use the "ideal type" method and thus to develop systems of categories that reflect the actual social world. Parsons terms this strategy "analytical realism," and he notes that it is necessary to develop a system of concepts that "adequately 'grasp' aspects of the objective external world—these concepts correspond not to concrete phenomena, but to elements in them

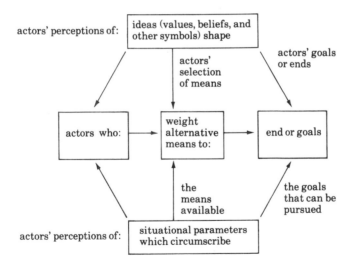

FIGURE 3.1 The Elements of Social Action

[17]It should be noted that Weber's ideal type method is very similar to taxonomic classification in biology—thus reviving Comte's vision of "social statics." *See* Jonathan H. Turner, *The Structure of Sociological Theory,* revised edition, (Homewood, Ill.: The Dorsey Press, 1978) for a more detailed argument along these lines.

which are analytically separable from other elements."[18] It is for this reason that Parsons develops a model containing the basic analytical elements of human action portrayed in Figure 3.1.

The other concern that drives Parsons toward functionalism is his recognition near the end of *The Structure of Social Action* that actors do not exist in isolation from each other. They interact within social systems, thus making his conceptual portrayal of the elements of individual action inadequate for describing systems of *inter*action. What is required is an additional, or more elaborate, system of concepts to grasp the basic properties of human social organization. The remainder of Parsons' intellectual career was to be devoted to elaborating a system of concepts that could "adequately grasp," and yet analytically accentuate, as Weber would appreciate, the key dimensions of complex patterns of human organization. And by 1945 Parsons has decided, along with others at Harvard, that functionalism is to provide a means for developing this conceptual taxonomy. As he noted:[19] "The structure of social systems cannot be derived directly from the actor-situation frame of reference. It requires *functional* analysis of the complications introduced by the interaction of a plurality of actors" (italics added). Thus, as Parsons has sought to capture the complexity of human organization, his conceptual taxonomy has been elaborated.[20] Much like a biologist, Parsons begins to invoke the concept of function and needs to order his conceptual categories. In many ways, then, Parsonian functionalism represents the ultimate effort as the realization of Comte's dream that "sociology would provide the basis of systematization for biology."[21]

THE FUNCTIONAL THEORY OF ACTION

Parsons' functionalism moves through two distinct phases: (a) the mechanism-equilibrium phase, and (2) the functional requisite phase. Since the second phase grows out of

---

[18]*The Structure of Social Action,* op. cit., p. 730.
[19]"Present Prospects . . .," op. cit., p. 229.
[20]Parsons was, of course, originally trained in biology. Moreover, the biologist, Walter Cannon, and physiologist, Lawrence J. Henderson, exert an influence on Parsons in his early years at Harvard.
[21]*See* Chapter 1.

the first and incorporates the mechanism-equilibrium analysis, it is best to examine each phase separately, especially if we are to appreciate the criticisms that Parsons' scheme inspired (see Chapter 5).

The Mechanism-Equilibrium Phase In 1951, two major works by Parsons and collaborators appeared: his *The Social System*[22] and the collaborative effort, *Toward a General Theory of Action.*[23] In these works, Parsons analytically separates three action systems: the cultural,[24] social, and personality (later he is to add a fourth, the organismic). The "cultural" is the system of symbols that is created and used by humans—an emphasis reminiscent of Malinowski's concern with symbols and "integrative needs" as well as of Parsons' own concern in *The Structure of Social Action* with the impact of "ideas" on individual action. The "social" is the system of relationships created out of interaction among individuals—again, an emphasis reminiscent of Radcliffe-Brown's and Malinowski's concern with institutions as emergent phenomena or Durkheim's insistence that society is a "social fact" and emergent reality, *sui generis.* The social system is thus the concept that Parsons is to employ in taking account of the fact that actors not only emit unit acts (see Figure 1) but they also *inter*act, forming stabilized patterns of social relations. The "personality" is the system of traits, such as needs, dispositions, cognitive states, and interpersonal skills that actors possess and draw upon as they interact with each other.

Parsons has, in many ways, simply elaborated each of the basic "elements of action" discussed in *The Structure of Social Action* into a "system of action." Ideas have become a cultural system; actors' goal-seeking and calculating activities are conceptualized as a "personality system"; and the missing element in the analysis of "unit acts," *inter*action, is now conceptualized as a "social system." The other elements of unit acts, biological and physical parame-

---

[22]Talcott Parsons, *The Social System* (New York: Free Press, 1951).

[23]Talcott Parsons, et al., *Toward a General Theory of Action* (New York: Harper & Row, 1951).

[24]Actually, in these early works Parsons only talks about "cultural patterns," but these soon are translated into a "cultural system."

ters, later become the fourth action system: the "organismic." (The reason Parsons added a fourth system will become evident when we analyze Parsons' analysis of four functional requisites.)

Thus, Parsons now visualizes human organization as composed of three analytically distinct systems: cultural, social, and personality. As a sociologist, he views the social system as the focal target of sociological analysis, but he recognizes that cultural symbols (ideas, beliefs, dogmas, technologies, language, and other symbolic components) and personality states (motives, cognitions, commitments, and skills) influence how actors interact in the social system. Thus, while the major task of sociological theory is to understand the process of institutionalization or the formation of stabilized social relations (that is, "social systems"), this understanding cannot occur without recognition of the impact of cultural symbols and personality components.

Much of *The Social System,* therefore, addresses the issue of how actors become committed and able to interact and how cultural patterns regulate interaction. Implicit in his analysis are two functional requisites: (1) The social system must have "a sufficient proportion of its component actors adequately motivated to act in accordance with the requirements of its role system."[25] (2) The social system must seek to avoid a situation in which cultural patterns "either fail to define a minimum of order or place impossible demands on people and thereby generate deviance and conflict."[26]

This concern leads Parsons to the analysis of "mechanisms" that assure that these two requisites are met. For Parsons, the operation of these mechanisms is what makes social systems possible. Conversely, the breakdown of these mechanisms will create instability and change in social systems.

Parsons begins to explore these mechanisms with a vocabulary which is, at best, unfortunate.[27] Borrowing from economic theory, especially from Pareto, and from analo-

[25] *The Social System,* op. cit., p. 27.
[26] Ibid., pp. 27–28.
[27] Parsons had received some training in economics, but his exposure to Pareto seems to have been decisive in his choice of concepts like equilibrium. Walter Cannon's notion of "homeostasis" (*The Wisdom of the Body,* New York: Norton and Company, 1939) also appears to have been crucial.

gies to biology and physics—to a degree reminiscent of Comte—Parsons creates an all-embracing image of social organization that is to become the object of severe, and often unfair, criticism. Parsons begins by asserting that for *analytical* purposes (not practical, empirical purposes, as his critics fail to recognize), a social system can be conceptualized as in "equilibrium." Analysis must then focus on the "mechanisms" that operate to maintain this equilibrium.

One set of mechanisms revolves around the integration of the personality system into the social system. There are two general classes of such mechanisms: (1) mechanisms of socialization and (2) mechanisms of social control. Mechanisms of socialization involve those processes in which (a) key cultural symbols are internalized by the personality system, (b) motives and skills for playing roles in the social system are acquired, and (c) strain and anxiety associated with learning and personality growth are mitigated.

Mechanisms of social control include the varied ways that positions and roles in the social system are organized so as to reduce conflict and tension. These mechanisms include: (a) institutionalization so that normative expectations on positions are clear, and potentially contradictory roles are segregated in time and space; (b) informal interpersonal sanctions to reduce deviance from expected behaviors; (c) ritual performances, from gestures of courtesy (such as handshakes) to symbolic enactment of religious rites, that release tensions and/or regularize interaction; (d) safety-valve organizations which allow widespread deviant dispositions to be enacted outside conventional patterns; (e) reintegration structures that seek to rehabilitate and resocialize deviants; and finally, (f) the concentration of power and the capacity for coercion so that order can be enforced.

These two general types of mechanisms for socialization and social control thus "resolve" the problem of assuring that actors are committed and able to play roles in the social system, and that they will continue to conform to normative expectations. Naturally, to the degree that these mechanisms are ineffective, the social equilibrium will be disrupted and social change will ensue. The other major requisite in Parsons' early functionalism concerns the integration of cultural patterns—values, beliefs, and other symbolic components—into the social system. Parsons does not explicitly name these processes as "mechanisms," but he clearly views systems of cultural symbols as operating as "mechanisms" to maintain the social equilibrium.

Parsons discusses two ways in which the cultural system performs this function. First, many components of culture, such as language, serve as resources for interaction. Without common symbolic resources, such as language, interaction in the social system could not occur. In this sense culture is a "facility." Second, following Durkheim's emphasis on "the collective conscience" and Max Weber's analysis of the impact of ideas on "social action,"[28] Parsons visualizes certain symbol systems as constraining and shaping the course of interaction. Such constraint occurs in at least two ways: Values, beliefs, and other symbolic components (a) give actors common assumptions with which to define situations and (b) provide them with instructions about how to act and interact.

Thus, Parsons' early functionalism follows Malinowski's and Radcliffe-Brown's distinction between social structure (the social system) and symbol systems (cultural system), and then, introduces a third action system, the personality.[29] His analysis at this point hinges on how some degree of integration is possible among these systems, and thus, he analyzes the mechanisms integrating these three distinctive system levels. Parsons' later functionalism retains this concern, but the place of requisites becomes more prominent and the scope of the scheme greatly expands.

The Requisite Functionalism Phase Parsons' functional approach develops rapidly after the 1951 publication of *The Social System* and *Toward a General Theory of Action.* The most important development involves the elaboration of four system requisites that all action systems—whether the cultural, social, personality, or organismic (which is added to the original three)—must meet if they are to survive.

---

[28]Parsons' exposure to, and subsequent translation of, Weber's *The Protestant Ethic and Spirit of Capitalism* appears to have been decisive.

[29]Contrary to many commentators' misreading (or lack thereof), the personality is not prominent in Malinowski's *theoretical* works. In some ethnographic works, such as *Magic, Science, and Religion* (Garden City, N.Y.: Doubleday, 1948), Malinowski is concerned with individuals and their psychological states.

These requisites,[30] virtually the same as Malinowski's four "derived needs" of social structure,[31] can be summarized as follows:

Adaptation:	All action systems must seek resources from the environment, convert them into usable facilities, and then distribute them to the rest of the system. This is the requisite of adaptation.
Integration:[32]	All action systems must maintain coherent interrelationships among their constituent parts, and inhibit tendencies for abnormalities in the relations among parts. This is the problem of integration.
Goal Attainment:[33]	All action systems must set goals, establish priorities and allocate resources in order to achieve them. This is the problem of goal attainment.
Latency:[34]	All action systems must (a) generate use units that can fit into the system (the problem of "pattern maintenance"), and (b) reduce tensions within units of the system ("tension management"). These combined problems are termed latency.

The elaboration of these requisites (abbreviated A, G, I, and L) simply represents extensions of ideas implicit in *The*

[30]The first clear statement appears in Talcott Parsons, Robert F. Bales, and Edward A. Shils, *Working Papers in the Theory of Action* (New York: Free Press, 1953).

[31]Parsons acknowledges his debt in an assessment of Malinowski's work. *See:* Talcott Parsons' "Malinowski and the Theory of Social Systems" in Raymond Firth's *Man and Culture* (London: Routledge and Kegan Paul, 1957).

[32]This emphasis follows from Parsons' concern with social systems and mechanisms of social control. See *The Social System*, op. cit.

[33]This emphasis follows, of course, from Parsons' emphasis that all action is goal directed. See *The Structure of Social Action*, op. cit.

[34]This concern follows from Parsons' emphasis in *The Social System* on the integration of personality and cultural systems into the social system, and on his discussion of the mechanisms of socialization and cultural integration.

Social System, and of course, ideas evident as early as 1937 in Malinowski's work. Yet, Parsons uses the concept of requisites to create an elaborate functional scheme. For any action system, substructures of the system can be analyzed in terms of which of the four requisites they meet. Since the social system is the primary concern of sociologists, the task of inquiry is to determine how various social structures (social systems)[35] meet their adaptive, goal attainment, integration, and latency needs. At the societal level, for example, dominant institutions would be first categorized in terms of which requisite they are most involved in meeting. Such an analysis would, of course, closely resemble Malinowski's analysis of "institutions" in relation to "derived needs."

Parsons goes much further than Malinowski, however. He begins to use diagrams for mapping the functional sectors of substructures within an action system and for tracing interrelations among and within structures of various

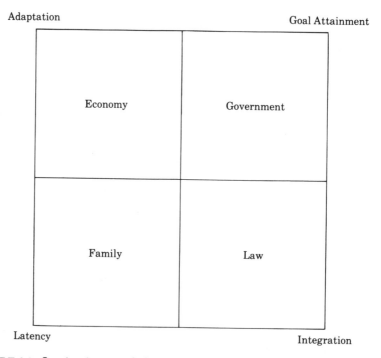

FIGURE 3.2   Institutions and the Societal Social System

[35]For Parsons, any institutionalized pattern is a "social system"—from a small group to an entire society, and even a system of societies.

sectors. Figure 3.2 presents a diagram of how Parsons might first categorize some of the institutions of a societal "social system."[36]

Then, Parsons would ask how, at the most analytical level, sectors involved in meeting one of the four requisites are interrelated with each other. Here, Parsons is seeking to discern the way subsystems interact within a more inclusive social system. Figure 3.3 presents a way that Parsons once visualized these exchanges between structures of the four functional sectors.[37]

Figures 3.2 and 3.3 only illustrate the application of what

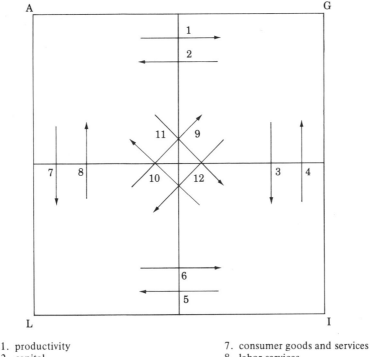

1. productivity
2. capital
3. imperative coordination
4. contingent support
5. pattern content
6. motivation to pattern conformity
7. consumer goods and services
8. labor services
9. new output combinations
10. entrepreneurial services
11. political loyalty
12. allocation of power

FIGURE 3.3 Interchanges of Subsystems and Functional Sectors of a Societal System

[36]For a detailed analysis following Parsons' lead, *see* Turner, *Patterns of Social Organization,* op. cit. The number of institutions listed in Figure 3.2 is, of course, not intended as exhaustive.

[37]*See* Talcott Parsons and Neil J. Smelser, *Economy and Society* (New York: Free Press, 1956), especially p. 68.

became known as the A, G, I, L scheme for institutions at the societal level. Actually, any social structure, such as the economy, also needs to meet the four functional problems. Thus, in an elaborate economy, one could expect to find discrete industries or corporations that are primarily involved in adaptation, goal attainment, integration, or latency. But of course each of these corporations, as discrete social systems in their own right, would also reveal A, G, I, L problems, and thus, if analysis were to focus on any one corporation, its different subparts—divisions, offices, etc.— could also be viewed as meeting primarily one or the other of the four requisites. The same would be true of a division within a corporation; it too could be analyzed in terms of the A, G, I, L framework. So could groups within divisions. Thus, as Figure 3.4 attempts to communicate for the adaptive sector of a social system—whether a society or some other system, such as a corporation—each constituent part is, in its own right also a social system, and thus amenable to analysis with the A, G, I, L scheme.

As can be seen, then, Parsons' requisite scheme argues for the utility of locating a subsystem's function, analyzing its

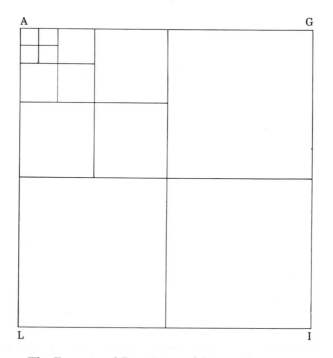

FIGURE 3.4   The Functional Requisites of Systems and Subsystems

relation to subsystems in other functional sectors, as well as discerning the A, G, I, L exchanges among its own constituent parts. Sociological theory, in this view, thus becomes an elaborate taxonomic and mapping operation in which the functions of structures are first classified and then interactions among functionally distinguished parts are traced.[38]

Parsons visualizes that social systems as well as cultural, psychological, and organismic action systems can be analyzed in this way. Moreover, Parsons retains the thrust of his first work, *The Structure of Social Action,* and the first functional work, *The Social System,* by using the A, G, I, L scheme to visualize an *overall* action system with the cultural, social, personality, and organismic systems as its constituent subsystems. Figure 3.5 presents his vision.

In this scheme, the organismic system (as the system providing energy to humans) resolves adaptive problems, the personality system (as the decision maker) deals with goal

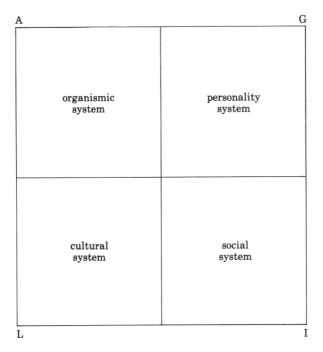

FIGURE 3.5 The Overall Action System

[38]We need not dwell on how biological analysis could have provided much of the inspiration for this form of functionalism.

attainment problems, the social system (as sets of relationships among actors) meets integrative problems, and the cultural system (as a system of symbols) handles latency problems. As with other analyses using the A, G, I, L scheme, Parsons then seeks to explore the relationships among all four systems (recall in *The Social System* that Parsons examined how mechanisms integrated culture and personality systems into the social system).

At this point, Parsons develops what he terms the "cybernetic hierarchy of control" to explore these relations among the subsystems of this overall action system.[39] Figure 3.6 presents this scheme. The basic idea is that systems high in "information," such as the cultural system (since, indeed, it is a system of symbols), provide regulation and control for systems lower in information but higher in energy. Thus, the symbols of the cultural system constrain and regulate interactions in social systems, the roles and positions of the social system circumscribe the action of the personality system, and internalized controls, such as the super-ego and other cognitive processes, influence many bodily functions of the organismic system. Conversely, systems high in energy provide the conditions and energic resources for systems higher in information. Thus, a personality system cannot exist without the energy from the human organism; the social system cannot exist without the drives and motives of the personality systems that play roles; and the cultural system's values, beliefs, language, and other symbolic components could not exist without the interactions in the social system that lead to the creation of symbols.

This scheme, Parsons feels, allows for much understanding of the dynamics of the social world. If there is an information or energy imbalance, certain consequences can be predicted. For example, if informational control from the cultural system is inadequate—a state that Durkheim termed "anomie"—then interaction in the social system will be disrupted. Or, if personality systems are

[39]*See* Talcott Parsons, "An Approach to Psychological Theory in Terms of the Theory of Action," in S. Koch, ed., *Psychology: A Science* (New York: McGraw-Hill, 1958). Talcott Parsons, "An Outline of the Social System" in T. Parsons, E. Shils, K. D. Naegele, and J. R. Pitts, eds., *Theories of Society* (New York: Free Press, 1961).

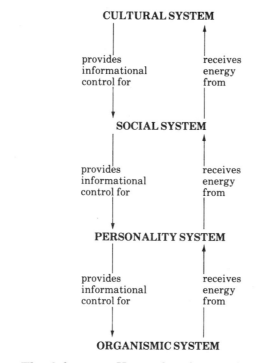

CULTURAL SYSTEM

provides
informational
control for

receives
energy
from

SOCIAL SYSTEM

provides
informational
control for

receives
energy
from

PERSONALITY SYSTEM

provides
informational
control for

receives
energy
from

ORGANISMIC SYSTEM

FIGURE 3.6   The Cybernetic Hierarchy of Control

unwilling to deposit energy in the roles of the social system, then a situation of alienation exists and interaction will be disrupted. Similar disruptive consequences could be predicted for information or energy imbalances between other systems. For example, a strong super-ego in the personality system can create guilt and anxiety (too much information) that in turn can lead to organic pathologies, such as high blood pressure and ulcers. Similarly, an insufficient calorie intake or organic disorder can cause disruption of the personality system.

Moreover, disruptions between any two action systems reverberate up and down the hierarchy. Lack of clarity over the values of the cultural system produces conflictual interaction in the social system; conflict mobilizes the personality system, creating tension and anxiety, and tension has clear psychological consequences for the organismic system. Conversely, insufficient calories can influence personality development which, in turn, has consequences for interaction in the social system that can influence the values and beliefs of the cultural system.

In recent years, Parsons has returned to his effort, outlined in Figure 3.3, to understand interchanges between sectors of only the social system. He has developed the concept of "generalized media of exchange" to conduct this analysis.[40] Basically, Parsons visualizes each functional sector of societal social systems as employing its own distinctive medium. Exchanges among subsystems of any sector are conducted in terms of a distinctive medium, and exchanges with subsystems of other functional sectors involve exchanges of one distinctive symbolic medium for another. For example, money is the symbolic medium of the adaptive sector, since adaptive subsystems conduct their affairs with money. And when adaptive subsystems exchange with subsystems of another sector, money is exchanged for the distinctive medium of that sector. For instance, the latency sector's symbolic medium is "commitments" to play roles, and thus, money comes from the economic organizations of the adaptive sector in exchange for the commitment on the part of households to perform labor. Parsons has yet to fully work out this scheme, but his intent is to begin examining the interrelations between functional sectors (diagrammed in Figure 3.3), or within a sector (as is illustrated in Figure 3.4) in terms of the distinctive media that they employ. Hence, the goal attainment sector's distinctive symbolic media is "power" (the capacity to induce or coerce conformity); the integrative sector's media is "influence" (the capacity to persuade); and as mentioned, the adaptive and latency sector's media, respectively, are "money" and "commitments."

[40]One can see in this concern of generalized media and its exchange Parsons' effort to abstract above the more concrete interchanges portrayed in Figure 3.3. *See* his: "On the Concept of Political Power," *Proceedings of the American Philosophical Society,* 107 (June, 1963):232–62; "On the Concept of Influence," *Public Opinion Quarterly,* 27 (Spring, 1963):37–62; and "Some Problems of General Theory" in J. C. McKinney and E. A. Tiryakian, eds., *Theoretical Sociology* (New York: Appleton-Century-Crofts, 1970), pp. 28–68. *See also* Talcott Parsons and Gerald Platt, *The American University* (Cambridge, Mass.: Harvard University Press, 1975).

PARSONS' FUNCTIONAL SCHEME: AN OVERVIEW

Much of the work of Comte, Spencer, Durkheim, Radcliffe-Brown, and Malinowski is embraced by Parsonian functionalism. The organismic analogy is retained in Parsons' tendency to employ taxonomies to analyze a structure in relation to function, and to map relations through the use of distinctive, symbolic (instead of chemical substances) media. Malinowski's concern with "basic needs" of the organism is given new life as the organismic system of an overall action system. Malinowski's and Radcliffe-Brown's separation of structures and symbols is incorporated into a distinction between the cultural and social systems. Malinowski's distinctions among system levels, and Durkheim's conception of society as a reality, *sui generis,* is preserved in the cybernetic hierarchy of control consisting of separable organismic, personality, social, and cultural systems. The emphasis of Durkheim and Radcliffe-Brown on integration is retained in the cybernetic hierarchy, but it is also emphasized in the integrative requisite of all action systems. Malinowski's analysis of four basic "derived needs" is borrowed and expanded to not just social systems, but to all action systems and to an overall action system.

In all of his analyses, of course, Parsons has merged other intellectual traditions from economics, psychology, anthropology, and sociology. More than any other social scientist of this century, Parsons has sought to cut across disciplines in order to unravel the mysteries of human action and organization. He has visualized functional analysis as the most fruitful perspective in this endeavor and his collective theoretical work represents the most complex and elaborate compendium of the functional schemes.

Parsons, we can argue, has taken functionalism to its logical conclusion as a *theoretical* strategy. And if this conclusion is found deficient, then functionalism as a theory building strategy is also deficient. This issue will be further explored in Chapters 5 and 6.

In contrast to its use in sociology, anthropological functionalism took a much different tack. Functionalism in anthropology concentrated on its use as a method for collecting and organizing the data base from which theory could be inducted and tested.

Functional Theory and Method in Anthropology

THE ETHNOGRAPHIC TRADITION

Functionalism in anthropology has, in many ways, concentrated on the analysis of individual societies, although the implicit intent has always been to create a data base for comparative analysis. Typically, the ethnographer examines critical traits of a system with reference to the functions that they have for the "survival," "maintenance," or "integration" of the system within a particular environment. For example, in a widely diverse set of essays presented in memory of Radcliffe-Brown,[41] a number of prominent anthropologists document, to varying degrees, the integrative functions of such diverse structures as rules of exogamy and incest, circumcision ceremonies, authority and public opinion, and governments and chiefs. All of these essays perform detailed structural analyses of the phenomenon under study, but each subtlety relates this analysis to what the structure "does for" the system in question. This, then, is the approach of anthropological functionalism: to interpret the functions of structures for the needs of individuals and the larger social whole. Systematic catalogues of needs are rarely presented; and apparently the cross-tabulation of structures and functions serves to explain why a structure exists and persists.

More functional analyses have been concerned with prominent structures, such as kinship rules, chiefdoms, law, and other core features of the society in question. In these cases the functional analysis does not distract from the structural description, since the descriptions appear to be done separately from the functional interpretation. One does not get a sense that ethnographers are using catalogues of survival "needs" to guide their descriptions of events. Only general notions that systems must be, to some unspecified degree, "integrated" and "insulated from the environment" appear to guide inquiry. Thus, the function of a structure is usually assessed in terms of these vaguely defined needs.

[41]Meyer Fortes, ed., *Social Structure: Studies Presented to A. R. Radcliffe-Brown* (New York: Russell and Russell, 1963).

Functionalism thus continues to be used as a way to view traditional societies as systemic wholes and to "understand" structures and processes without delving into their historical past and without invoking notions of evolution or diffusion. At times, however, functional arguments are phrased in terms of "social selection." For example, Stuart Piddocke's analysis of the Potlatch ceremonies of the Southern Kwakiutl provides an illustration of this approach. The Potlatch, a ceremony that has long fascinated anthropologists, is one in which individuals from different groups compete to give away valuable goods to each other. It is the ultimate display of ostentation as members of the Kwakiutl compete and try to outdo each other in their gift giving. The more that is given, and the more valuable the gifts, the more prestige to the giver. The "winner" in this competition is the one who is able to give more than is received.

Piddocke[42] develops a functional argument to explain this seemingly "strange" custom:

1. In the past, scarcity among some groups of Kwakiutl created problems of survival for subpopulations.
2. The Potlatch of these early times was confined to the chiefs of local kinship groups.
3. Through the competition among chiefs "wealth objects," such as canoes, slaves, and blankets, could be exchanged for the food resources needed by a group with a scarcity of food.
4. In this way, the level of subsistence among all Kwakiutl was maintained, with those having to give wealth objects for food receiving prestige for doing so (thus, presumably avoiding the degradation of begging for food, or the disruption of attempting to take it by force). Naturally, to have received wealth objects in exchange for food allows the recipient at another time to give them away for prestige, or for food (if needed).
5. This rivalry among chiefs for prestige was adopted by the general population in later times, thus assuring the flow of vital food resources.

[42]Stuart Piddocke, "The Potlatch System of the Southern Kwakiutl: A New Perspective" in A. P. Vayda, ed., *Environment and Cultural Behavior* (Garden City, N.Y.: Natural History Press, 1969), pp. 130–156.

As Martin Orans points out,[43] there are a number of substantive errors in Piddocke's interpretation of Kwakiutl history. For the present, however, our concern is with the form of Piddocke's argument (which as we shall see in Chapter 6, Orans also questions). Piddocke's argument is basically a social selection thesis: The Potlatch had adaptive value in allowing the Kwakiutl to preserve their entire population, even when some groups faced extinction through starvation. The Potlatch was thus "selected" and retained because it facilitated, and now promotes, survival.

Such an argument, of course, violates both Radcliffe-Brown's and Malinowski's dictum of not delving into the unknown past. Moreover, the argument cannot be put to a test, since the historical record is unclear. It thus represents speculation, dressed up in a kind of social selection imagery, about what the Potlatch "does for" the Kwakiutl.

We can see, then, that the ethnographic tradition in anthropology has employed functionalism as a kind of ad hoc tool for "making sense" of particular cultural items. This *is* the extent of functional *theory* in anthropology: limited, ad hoc "explanations" of particular social structures and events in terms of their functions for ill-defined needs—survival, integration, and maintenance. This line of theorizing is clearly within Radcliffe-Brown's tradition, as he illustrated with the Andaman Islanders[44] and his various discussions of kinship.

Lost in this approach is Malinowski's more elaborate conceptual edifice of examining types of institutions in terms of their structural features (charter, personnel, material apparatus, and norms) as well as their functions in meeting derived needs, whether these be the four instrumental or three integrative needs. Also lost is the vision of both Radcliffe-Brown and Malinowski that functional analysis could provide an approach for comparing social systems and thus inducting the general laws of human organization.

It is this failure to use functionalism as a method for comparative analysis that has led Walter Goldschmidt to develop an alternative functional approach. This approach

---

[43]Martin Orans, "Domesticating the Functional Dragon: An Analysis of Piddocke's Potlatch," *American Anthropologist,* 77 (1975):312–327.

[44]A. R. Radcliffe-Brown, *The Andaman Islanders* (Glencoe, Ill.: Free Press, 1948).

would, in Goldschmidt's eyes, correct for the tendency to perform functional analyses of single cultures. At the same time it would rekindle a concern with comparative analysis, while avoiding problems that Goldschmidt perceives to exist in Malinowski's comparative approach.

COMPARATIVE FUNCTIONALISM: WALTER GOLDSCHMIDT'S APPROACH

As functional analysis became increasingly attuned to assessing the functions of social structures for individual cultures, Walter Goldschmidt in the mid-1960s sought to recapture the comparative thrust of the functional method.[45] As the custodians of a particular body of data on traditional peoples, Goldschmidt argues, anthropologists have an obligation to present this data, and to provide reasonable interpretations of its meaning, to the social sciences. To meet this obligation, anthropology must focus on the consistencies that can be observed across cultures, for only with attention to these matters can the theoretical importance of anthropological activity for developing a theory of human behavior and social organization be realized.

As Marx did for Hegel, Goldschmidt "turns Malinowski on his head," arguing that social institutions are highly variable, while many of the problems that humans face are universal. These universal problems, therefore, should provide the basis for the comparative analysis of social systems.

The Malinowskian Dilemma Goldschmidt presents his alternative method of functionalism as a solution to an inherent dilemma: To examine individual cultures in detail makes comparisons among cultures different. Since each social system exists in, and has adapted to, a somewhat unique environment, it will have developed structural patterns that differ in detail from those of a system that persists in a different environment. Since ethnographic methods, as personified by Malinowski's extensive description of the Trobriand Islanders,[46] will by necessity focus on structural

---

[45]Walter Goldschmidt, *Comparative Functionalism* (Berkeley: University of California Press, 1966).

[46]*See,* for example: Bronislaw Malinowski, *Argonauts of the Western Pacific* (London: Routledge and Kegan Paul, Ltd., 1922). *Sex and Repression in Savage Society* (London: Routledge and Kegan Paul, Ltd., 1927).

patterns of an individual culture, it will be difficult to have a "common yardstick" for comparing varying structural patterns. While Malinowski hoped that the delineation of common elements of all social institutions—personnel charter, norms, marital apparatus, and function—and the listing of universal institutions (see Table 1 in Chapter 2) would provide a basis for comparing structural patterns across cultures, Goldschmidt argues against such a strategy.

His alternative strategy stresses that social structures are rarely comparable. Indeed, an institution such as kinship can vary enormously, forcing the comparison of noncomparables. Moreover, comparison can lead to a constant process of redefining institutions so as to incorporate each additional case. For example, Goldschmidt documents how one analyst[47] of the Nayar is forced to redefine the institution of marriage in order to view the somewhat unique and extreme practices of the Nayar as "marriage." Comparative analyses soon lose their focus when the yardstick for making comparisons must constantly be recalibrated.

In sum, then, Goldschmidt views the concept of institution as an inappropriate yardstick for comparative analysis. While the description of institutionalized social patterns is essential in generating an ethnographic report on an individual culture, it will not serve as a basis for the comparative analysis of diverse social systems. To resolve this dilemma it is necessary to use functions as the yardstick for comparison.

Institutionalization and Functional Problems   Goldschmidt argues that anthropology must view social structures as a verb rather than as a noun. Instead of studying static and discrete institutions, attention should focus on the process of *institutionalization.* In this way, human action and organization can be seen as a process of adaptation to problems that confront all human populations. While institutionalized patterns have common elements[48]—personnel,

---

[47]Kathleen Gough, "The Najars and the Definition of Marriage" in P. Bohannan's and J. Middleton's *Marriage, Family, and Residence* (Garden City, N.Y.: Natural History Press, 1968).

[48]We should note how similar to Malinowski's institutional elements are Goldschmidt's.

boundaries, organization, symbolic integration, patterned and external relations—these cannot be the yardstick of comparison, because of the wide variability in *how* they function to meet the biological, psychological, and social contingencies of human existence.

Anthropological analysis must therefore address the questions: What universal needs confront humans? And how have different populations of humans, living in different environments under varying historical circumstances, resolved similar problems? The task of anthropological theory thus becomes one of isolating some of the basic problems confronting all populations of humans and then comparing social systems in terms of how they have institutionalized solutions to these problems. The solutions will, of course, vary from system to system, but now these varying institutionalized patterns can be compared as responses to a common problem. The comparison of institutionalized solutions to common problems thus resolves the "Malinowskian dilemma."

Functional Requisites Goldschmidt does not present a list or catalogue of "problems" that all human systems must meet. Such a list, Goldschmidt appears to argue,[49] can too easily become rigid, forcing reality into its mold. For example, to postulate one functional requisite as Durkheim and Radcliffe-Brown did (the need for integration), soon compels analysts to view structures as having only one consequence. Expanding the list of requisites can, of course, help alleviate this difficulty, but to become prematurely committed to any exhaustive list of universal requisites, as did Parsons or Malinowski, can tempt analysts to view reality by the dictates of their list of a priori requisites rather than by the real problems of actual peoples. Goldschmidt also appears to distrust lists because they can obscure the fact that social systems at different stages of development or structural elaboration may have created new requisites that less developed systems do not reveal. While certain requisites are universal and inherent in being human and in the necessity of social collaboration, the nature of the collabora-

---

[49]Goldschmidt is a bit vague on just why a comprehensive list is not developed and thus, we must often infer his rationale.

tion can involve elaboration of requisites necessary to maintain extended patterns of social organization. For instance, Goldschmidt discusses the "contingent functions" of statecraft or statehood as a way of providing a common analytical measure of systems revealing elaborated political activities. Thus, he offers a summary of contingent functions which systems evidencing patterns of centralized political authority must meet. Yet, Goldschmidt appears ambiguous about whether such contingent functions are requisites, for "we must remember that contingent functions are not requisites in an absolute sense, and thus may not be requisite at all."[50] Indeed, for many simple systems, such elaborated functions need not be met, since collaborative efforts are not sufficiently complex.

The key point is that contingent functions introduce a new complexity to comparative functionalism. Moreover, they make the construction of exhaustive lists of requisites artificial, since it is entirely possible that further collaborative efforts can create new contingent functions.[51] Comparative functionalism must therefore remain open to the necessity of constructing new statements on contingent functions. Thus, if social systems reveal elaborated and still highly variable political structures, then an abstract statement of the contingent functions must be constructed to provide a standard for comparing variations in this structural elaboration.

Goldschmidt does not claim, however, that such lists are useless. On the contrary, they are the central focus of the functional approach. What he implicitly stresses is that claims as to exhaustiveness of any list are, at present, premature. With continued search for universal requisites and with their use in comparative analysis, a core list of requisites may eventually be constructed. For the moment, Goldschmidt seems more concerned with illustrating the utility of the approach than with postulating a closed analytical system.

He does, however, suggest two general problems that all human systems confront. One problem concerns the needs that collective patterns of social organization must resolve

---

[50]*Comparative Functionalism*, op. cit., p. 116.
[51]We might note that Goldschmidt's approach is similar to Max Weber's ideal-type method.

if they are to endure. The other concerns the integration of individual actors with their own distinctive sense of self-identity and other psychological and biological attributes into the collective. Humans cannot survive without patterns of social organization to meet basic biological and psychological needs, but once created these patterns reveal their own needs (this is, of course, Malinowski's emphasis in his distinction between "primary" and "derived" needs). But humans, by virtue of their biological wants and their symbolic capacities to create a sense of self-identity, can potentially be placed in conflict with the needs of the collective, and hence, there is a requisite for self-collectivity integration.[52]

Thus, Goldschmidt suggests that it is around these basic requisites that other more specific needs will cohere. What is it that humans need to survive biologically and psychologically? And what new needs are created by the fact of social organization and by the need to integrate individuals with biological and psychological needs into these patterns?

Examples of Comparative Functionalism   Since Goldschmidt has avoided constructing a catalogue of requisites, we can only illustrate his approach with the examples that he supplies. One example comes from his criticism of those who have sought to describe variations in marriage patterns. Rather than juggle definitions of marriage to fit variable social patterns, we should focus on the functions that marriage, family, and related social patterns serve. In this way a more systematic recording of the variations across cultures in terms of how they have resolved a universal set of problems is possible. Hence, Goldschmidt provides the following list of functions:[53]

1. Delineation of rights to sexual access, including the public presentation of those rights and sanctions against breach.
2. Provision for the nurture of infants and care of pregnant and lactating mothers, including the definitions of rights and obligations. . . .

[52]This is an issue which Parsons' early formulation of the pattern variables emphasized.
[53]*Comparative Functionalism,* op. cit., pp. 93–94.

3. Provision of a defined social status and social identity for the child.

4. Provision of education and indoctrination of the child. . . .

5. Provision of an identification object for both parents through which they may project themselves into the future through sociologically established descendants.

Functions (1) through (5) must be met if a system is to survive. Just *how* populations have resolved these universal problems has, of course, been highly variable. By examining cultural patterns in relation to universal functions, this variability can be compared to a common point of reference.

These functions are clear requisites in that all systems must resolve them to remain viable. As we noted, however, Goldschmidt also develops the concept of "contingent functions" to order the comparison of elaborated social structures. For example, to provide the common reference point for cultures with differentiated political systems, he proposes the following list of functions:[54]

1. The establishment of roles defining the rights and obligations of the authority center.
   a. The transmission of these roles to new incumbents
   b. Sanctions supporting these roles
   c. Symbolic representation of these roles

2. The articulation system between the authority center and the personnel
   a. The location of lines of communication between the center and peripheries
   b. The sanctions for intermediate role positions
   c. The containment of these intermediaries so as to prevent usurpation of power

3. The provision of conflict resolution mechanisms
   a. Among citizens or constituent groups
   b. Between such citizens or groups and the center of authority

4. The provision of protection against external threats to the structure

[54]Ibid., pp. 114–115.

5. Economic support of the authority system itself, and of its personnel

In sum, then, Goldschmidt is concerned with comparative analysis—that is, with using the large body of accumulative data for theoretical purposes. This was Malinowski's vision, and to a lesser degree, Radcliffe-Brown's.[55] But this vision over the last decades became obscured with concern over detailed ethnographies of individual cultures and with efforts to compare noncomparables. Goldschmidt thus views his comparative functionalism as an alternative method for bringing conceptual and analytical order to anthropological data.

Modern Functionalism: An Overview

In this chapter, we have reviewed the range of functional approaches, and some of their major proponents. All of these approaches are indebted to the creators of functionalism—Comte, Spencer, and Durkheim—and to the two anthropologists who preserved the functional tradition—Radcliffe-Brown and Malinowski.

Among anthropologists, functionalism has tended to be viewed as a method for organizing data, while among sociologists the emphasis has been on functionalism as an explanatory theory. Some, such as Robert Merton and, we suspect, Walter Goldschmidt, view functionalism as a way to present and organize data and also as a procedure for explaining why social systems should evidence certain regularities. But if we look closely at the written record, it is clear that scholars tend to stress either the methodological or explanatory utility of functionalism.

Both points of emphasis have been severely criticized, and thus, we must review the problems inherent in the functional orientation, whether as a method or theory. Before we do so, however, it might be wise to summarize the vision of social reality that the functional orientation has developed. For indeed this general vision has been as often criticized as the specific details of its methodological and

[55]It was, of course, the vision of many others, including George Murdock, *Social Structure* (New York: Macmillan Co., 1949) and his HARF files.

theoretical procedures. Moreover, in addition to presenting an often criticized element in the functional approach, we can also sum up our discussion in the preceding chapters and lay the groundwork for assessing the problems and prospects of functionalism in the social sciences.

4

Methods and Models of Functionalism

Functionalism has been used as both a theoretical orientation and as a method for collecting data. These two facets of functionalism are, of course, interrelated since the use of functionalism as a data collection strategy also implies a scheme for interpreting the data. Conversely, theoretical schemes dictate certain ways of collecting information in order to test their implications.

Yet, it is still useful to separate these two facets of functionalism and view them as different points of emphasis within a general theoretical tradition. Accordingly, we will first explore some of the theoretical assumptions of models of functionalists, and then, review the various functional methodologies.

Functional Assumptions and Models

Some authors, such as Kingsley Davis,[1] argue against the view that functionalism in the social sciences represents a distinctive theoretical approach. This argument asserts that all sociological inquiry (a) examines humans within a systemic context; (b) seeks to discover why variations in systems can be accounted for by variations in constituent parts; and at the same time (c) attempts to discover why

[1]Kingsley Davis, "The Myth of Functional Analysis as a Special Method of Sociology," *American Sociological Review,* 10 (December, 1959):759.

certain social patterns are universal. Davis believes that while some scholars use terms like "meets the needs of" or "has the function of," they are engaged in essentially the same intellectual activity as those who use other terms to capture the systemic properties of human action and organization.

This argument, we feel, is incorrect.[2] Functionalism is a unique way of looking at the social world and interpreting events in this world. This fact can best be demonstrated by reviewing the varieties of functional approaches, highlighting in each what makes them "functional."

THE MINIMAL FUNCTIONAL MODEL

While Comte and Spencer must be credited with bringing the organismic analogy, and its functional trappings, into sociology, Émile Durkheim was the first to advocate an explicitly functional set of assumptions:[3]

1. A social system must reveal some degree of internal integration among its constituent parts.
2. The important theoretical task is to determine the consequences, or functions, of a constituent part for the integration of the systemic whole.
3. The "causes" of a part must be analyzed separately from its "functions" for social integration.

These assumptions are represented in Figure 4.1. They can be visualized as the most minimal features of functional analysis. They contain both a method and an implicit

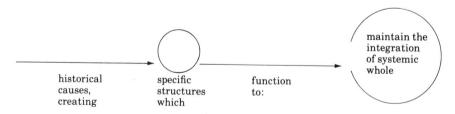

FIGURE 4.1 The Minimal Functional Model

[2]For a more thorough review of this argument, *see* Jonathan H. Turner, "The Future of Functionalism" in *The Structure of Sociological Theory*, revised edition (Homewood, Ill.: The Dorsey Press, 1978).

[3]*See* especially, Émile Durkheim, *The Rules of the Sociological Method* (New York: Free Press, 1930, originally published 1895).

theory. Methodologically, Durkheim stresses that the examination of a system part, such as the division of labor or
religious ritual (see Chapter 1), must involve a two-fold process: a separate search for its historical causes and an investigation into its present functions. This latter directive
implies a theory of human organization, leading to an additional assumption:

    4. The need for social integration operates as a selective
       mechanism for the persistence of those parts that pro-
       mote integration of the social whole.

This fourth assumption disturbed Durkheim, for he recognized the dangers of illegitimate teleology.[4] How can the
end result (social integration) produce its cause (division of
labor)? The only way to avoid such an argument is to employ, as Durkheim implicitly did, a social selection assumption: Those traits, whatever the reason for their initial
emergence, that facilitate survival (i.e., social integration)
will be retained, while those that do not will be "selected
out" of a system. This model is summarized in Figure 4.2.

    Figure 4.2 begins to move functional theory more explic-
itly toward the analysis of functional requisites and away
from the analysis of historical causes. Durkheim would
have insisted, of course, that historical analysis was essential, but those anthropologists who were the first to use
Durkheim's functional approach were disinclined toward
historical analysis.[5]

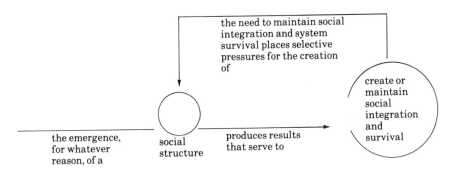

FIGURE 4.2 The Social Selection Model

  [4]See, Émile Durkheim, *The Division of Labor in Society* (New York: Free
Press, originally published in 1893).
  [5]See our discussion in Chapter 2 on "The Preservation of Functionalism."

ANTHROPOLOGICAL FUNCTIONALISM

Radcliffe-Brown's Functional Model   For Radcliffe-Brown, functional analysis involves the search for the "sociological origin" (as opposed to historical origin) of a structure for the maintenance of integration of the social whole. Thus, Radcliffe-Brown did not heed Durkheim's directive to separate causal and functional analysis. The result is a functional model that becomes decidedly circular: The sociological explanation of a structure resides in the determination of its function in meeting integrative needs.[6] In this argument the only way to avoid charges of tautology is to employ, as Radcliffe-Brown implicitly does, a social selection process: those structures that persist have been able to resolve certain "necessary conditions of existence"—that is, the integrative needs of the social whole. Thus, Radcliffe-Brown's functional model abandons Durkheim's methodological dictates of separate causal and functional analysis. This model is summarized in Figure 4.3.

Much of the ethnographic functional analysis, discussed in the last chapter, employs this model. Specific structures, such as incest taboos, kinship patterns, and religious rituals are examined in terms of their "functions" for maintaining either the internal integration of the social whole or its survival and persistence in a given environment. Rarely is the implicit social selection argument invoked, although we noted in Chapter 3 that Piddocke's analysis of the Potlatch employs a selective argument: the Potlatch has selective advantage in allowing the distribution of food

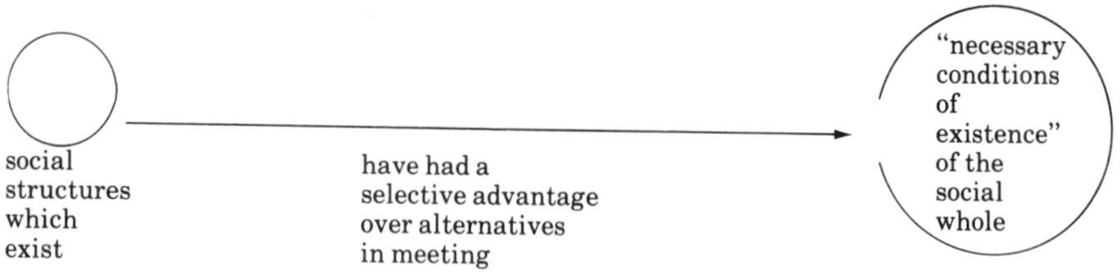

social
structures
which
exist

have had a
selective advantage
over alternatives
in meeting

"necessary
conditions
of
existence"
of the
social
whole

FIGURE 4.3   The Ahistorical Functional Model

[6]*See,* for example, A. R. Radcliffe-Brown, *Structure and Function in Primitive Society* (London: Cohen and West, 1952).

resources to subpopulations which otherwise might starve, thereby maintaining the entire Kwakiutl population.

Malinowski's Functional Model   As we noted in Chapter 2 Malinowski views his brand of functionalism as a heuristic way to organize, rather than interpret, data. Yet, he employs a set of theoretical assumptions in his functionalism:[7]

1.   Humans have basic or primary needs which prompt them to become collectively organized in order to meet their needs.
2.   Once humans are collectively organized, their collaboration creates new, "derived" needs.
3.   These needs can only be met by the creation and maintenance of certain institutional patterns.
4.   To understand the "reasons" for the existence of a social structure it is necessary to determine its functions for either basic or derived needs.

In the fourth assumption, we should note the vagueness of the word, "reasons." Malinowski is not completely clear as to whether or not the assessment of the function of an institution is an explanation of that institution or simply a heuristic device for its description. Malinowski at least implies, especially in his ethnographic work, that a selective mechanism is involved in the establishment and preservation of an institution. The "reason" for the existence and persistence of an institution is that, from whatever causes, it emerged and resolved basic and derived needs—thereby assuring its persistence. His model is diagrammed in Figure 4.4.

Malinowski's model is more complex than Durkheim's or Radcliffe-Brown's, because he explicitly introduces and maintains distinctions among three levels of reality:[8] the organismic, the institutional or social structural, and the symbolic. Contrary to almost every discussion and critique of Malinowski, we should emphasize that he does *not*, in his

[7]*See,* in particular, Bronislaw Malinowski, *A Scientific Theory of Culture and Other Essays* (Chapel Hill: University of North Carolina Press, 1944).

[8]Radcliffe-Brown's emphasis upon "culture" as social structure implicitly argues for the distinction between at least the structural and symbolic levels. Durkheim's stress on the "collective conscience" is separated from actual structure patterns, such as the division of labor, similarly implies this distinction between a structural and symbolic level. Yet, it is Malinowski who makes this, and other distinctions, explicitly a part of his theoretical scheme.

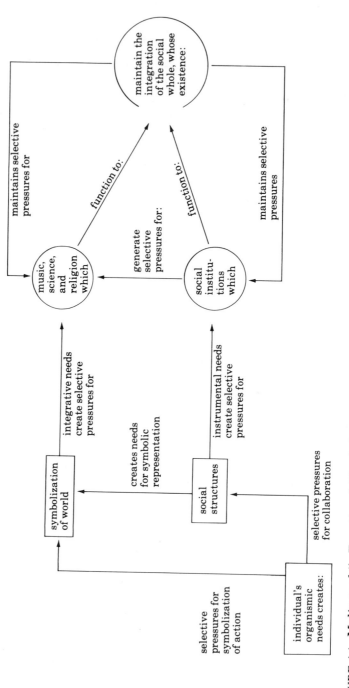

FIGURE 4.4 Malinowski's Functional Needs Model

formal theoretical model, address the individual and psychological needs. Scholars have consistently misinterpreted Malinowski on this score.[9] Yet, Malinowski's willingness to address the issue of needs or requisites at different system levels opened new analytical possibilities: The operation of social structures must be analyzed not only in terms of their own requisites, but also in terms of the degree to which the needs of other system levels impose constraints on how social structural systems can meet their requisites. It is this analytical level that Parsons was to elaborate into two different types of functional models: the mechanism-equilibrium model and the requisite functions model.

PARSONS' MECHANISM-EQUILIBRIUM MODEL

In *The Social System,*[10] Talcott Parsons becomes concerned with how the equilibrium of the social system is maintained by the operation of mechanisms to integrate both cultural patterns and personality systems into the stabilized patterns of interaction that make up social systems. Unlike Malinowski, however, Parsons maintains his focus on the social system and only addresses the issue of integration of culture and personality *into* the social system. He does not, at this stage of his thinking, speculate extensively about how requisites of the cultural or personality systems impose constraints on patterns of social organization in the social system. Such actions are left implicit, allowing him to concentrate on mechanisms integrating culture and personality into the social system. This early mechanism-equilibrium model is presented in Figure 4.5.[11]

In this analysis, then, social structures are assessed in terms of which mechanism they personify. The purpose of such assessment is to analyze how a structure, as an instance of more general mechanisms, operates to promote social equilibrium (and conversely, how its failure to operate "properly" would produce disequilibrium and change).

[9]The only explanation for this misinterpretation is Malinowski's ethnographic work which, as a description of people's lives and living patterns, addresses individuals. But in his theoretical works, Malinowski is explicit about his concern with social structure and derived needs.

[10]Talcott Parsons, *The Social System* (New York: The Free Press, 1951).

[11]Adapted from Jonathan H. Turner, *The Structure of Sociological Theory,* revised edition, op. cit., p. 102.

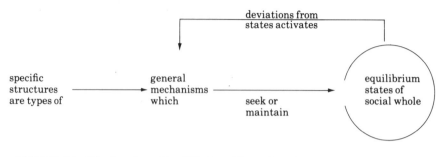

FIGURE 4.5   Mechanism-Equilibrium Functional Analysis

REQUISITE FUNCTIONALISM IN SOCIOLOGY
The analysis of requisites and needs in sociological theory does not invoke as explicitly as is the case in anthropology the notion of "social selection" of traits. Since sociologists tend to study modern societies where survival against the forces of nature *seems* less problematic, and where political systems often create structures for explicit purposes, concern with how a structure is "selected for" by virtue of its capacity to facilitate survival is less central to theoretical models. Instead, concern appears to be with establishing an exhaustive list of *general* functional needs and then examining structures in terms of their consequences for meeting these needs. Much of the functionalism appears to involve simply using notions of requisites as a way of categorizing structures, and then, analyzing interchanges among structures so categorized. Again, this propensity can perhaps be explained by the fact that sociologists study more differentiated social systems than anthropologists. Indeed, the social systems studied by sociologists tend to reveal a clearly separated economy, polity, kinship pattern, legal system, educational facility, and religious system. It is thus easy to view separable structures as meeting distinguishable system requisites.

Talcott Parsons'[12] early functional requisite model postulates four social system requisites and then analyzes subsystems, and their interrelations, in terms of which requisite they are primarily involved in meeting. This early requisite model is outlined in Figure 4.6.

Parsons' later requisite functionalism appears to ap-

---

[12]Parsons' requisite model is much like that developed by other sociologists of this period, such as Kingsley Davis and Marion J. Levy.

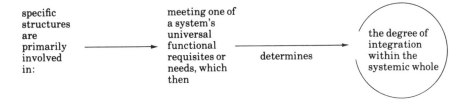

FIGURE 4.6 Requisite Functionalism in Sociology

proach the spirit, if not the substance, of Malinowski's model. Parsons begins to view four system levels, each meeting one of four system requisites in an overall action system. In turn, each system level—the organismic, personality, social, and cultural—must meet these same four needs, as must any of their subsystems. Whereas Malinowski postulated different requisites for each system level, Parsons moves up the abstraction ladder in order to view all action systems and subsystems as being required to meet the same four requisites. Specific components of personality, particular biological operations, each institutional pattern, or a given symbolic code are all to be examined in relation to which of the four requisites of their respective systems—whether the personality, organismic, social, or cultural—each subpart meets.

But Parsons also becomes intrigued with interrelations among the four subsystems (organismic, personality, social, and cultural) of the overall action system. This is represented in his presentation of the cybernetic hierarchy of control (see Chapter 3). It also becomes evident in his more recent work on social evolution.[13] In general, he views the outputs of one system level as being inputs to another, with insufficient or excessive inputs creating problems for meeting a given set of requisites for a system. For example, if personality inputs—commitment and ability to play roles—into the social system are insufficient, then the requisites of that system cannot be met. Similar deficiencies, or excesses, of information of energy pose problems for meeting requisites of other action systems. Thus, in Figure 4.6, if we view the "systemic whole" as an overall action system and "spe-

[13]Talcott Parsons, *Societies: Evolutionary and Comparative Perspectives* (Englewood Cliffs, N.J.: Prentice-Hall, 1966) and *The System of Modern Societies* (Englewood Cliffs, N.J.: Prentice-Hall, 1971).

cific structures" as one of the four action systems, we can see that Parsons' more recent analysis is much the same as his earlier requisite functionalism, only grander in scope.

THE "NET BALANCE OF FUNCTIONS" MODEL

Robert Merton initially developed his functional paradigm in reaction to Malinowski's scheme, although it would not be difficult to visualize his strategy as an alternative to Parsons' even grander scheme.[14] For Merton, the essential feature of functionalism is the emphasis on the consequences of a social structure for different system referents, whether the individual, another structure, or the systemic whole. In this assessment of consequences, attention can be drawn to needs or requisites, but these must be *empirically* established for each system referent. Merton then advocates an assessment of the net balance of functions of a specific structure. Merton's model is thus clearly a method for analysis, with only secondary thought to the use of the concept of function as an explanatory principle. He argues:

1. Functional analysis must concern empirical systems, not abstract systems.
2. Investigation must focus on a particular structural pattern of interest.
3. This structural pattern must be assessed in terms of its consequences for *empirically* determined requisites (not a priori, abstract needs) of the system in which it is implicated and of the individuals in the system.
4. Functional analysis must assess the positive, negative, and nonfunctional consequences of a structure on empirically established requisites.
5. By careful performance of number 4 above, the "net balance of consequences" of a structure can be assessed.
6. Understanding the net balance of functions can allow for the development of abstract generalizations about limited ranges of phenomena.[15]

[14]Robert K. Merton, "Manifest and Latent Functions" in his *Social Theory and Social Structure* (New York: Free Press, 1949).
[15]*See* Robert K. Merton, "On Sociological Theories of the Middle Range" in his *Social Theory and Social Structure* (New York: Free Press, 1968).

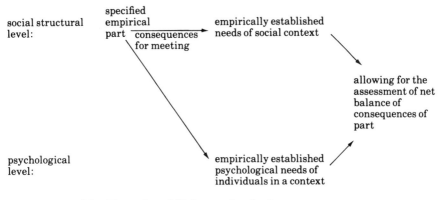

FIGURE 4.7   Net Functional Balance Analysis

In Figure 4.7, we have presented Merton's net balance of functions model.[16]

Functional Methods and Strategies

Central to all functionalisms is the notion that understanding functions gives investigators clues as to what are important social processes and structures in social systems. Those structures and processes which are "vital" to system "integration" and "survival" will constitute more crucial topics of study than those which are not as necessary for meeting basic requisites. The corollary assumption to this argument is that only by examination of these functionally important structures will it be possible to formulate the "laws" of human organization. Thus, in addition to constituting a metaphysical view of the world, functionalism also represents a methodological strategy for generating data, and ordering this data, so that true theory can be built and tested. Before closing this chapter, then, we ought to review briefly this aspect of functionalism.

For both Radcliffe-Brown and Malinowski, functionalism represents a method that will allow synchronic analysis and avoid the methodological problems of historical analysis among social systems without a written history. Thus, Durkheim's functionalism is dramatically altered

[16]Adapted Turner, *The Structure* ..., revised edition, op. cit., p. 103.

since, as can be recalled, Durkheim advocated a separate causal (historical) and functional analysis.

Malinowski goes further than Radcliffe-Brown and uses lists of biological needs and derived needs as a way to highlight the functions of social institutions. Malinowski advocates a comparative method in which universal institutions are to be the yardstick for comparing diverse cultures. Thus, while Malinowski employs the concept of function as a background assumption for understanding *why* institutions should exist (they meet basic and derived needs), he does not use the concept as a key element in his comparative method.

Subsequent scholars, however, were to make the concept of need and function a central methodological tool. As is outlined in Figure 4.7, Merton argues that empirically established system requisites and individual needs are useful tools for tracing out the consequences of social structures on systemic wholes, subsystems, and individuals. But the notion of requisites and needs must be established for each system under investigation, since Merton feels that a priori assumptions about universal needs and requisites will bias and distort empirical investigation.

Talcott Parsons and other sociologists have not followed Merton's lead and have sought to construct exhaustive lists of universal requisites. Parsons' scheme uses the four requisites of all action systems as a methodological tool for sorting out crucial social processes: those structures critical for meeting adaptive, goal attainment, integrative or latency needs are the most important topics of investigation.[17] Parsons also employs the notion of system requisites as a means for categorizing social structures and then examining the relations among structures as categorized. For example, by locating a structure in the adaptive sector Parsons can systematically trace its relationships to other structures located within the three other sectors of an action system.

The anthropologist, Walter Goldschmidt,[18] has developed a functionalism that has eschewed all these tendencies of

[17]Parsons' many insightful essays on a wide variety of substantive topics might well attest to how well he has used his own scheme as a method for investigating concrete empirical events.

[18]Walter Goldschmidt, *Comparative Functionalism* (Berkeley: University of California Press, 1966).

sociologists. His scheme leaves open the question of discovering a closed system of universal requisites, but it also views certain requisites as universal for all populations of humans. Moreover, he does not use requisites as a way to categorize and locate social structures within a grand analytical scheme. Rather, in "turning Malinowski on his head," he uses the concept of requisites as a way of comparing social structures across cultures. By isolating certain universal (and contingent) problems that humans and human systems must resolve, and then by comparing cultures in terms of how they evolve and elaborate structures to resolve these problems, it is possible to present systematic comparisons of human social systems—thereby creating a data set amenable to theory building and testing.

In sum, then, we can visualize a wide diversity of functional methods. The common element in all these approaches is the assumption that the assessment of needs and requisites provides a useful tool for "getting a handle" on a complex empirical world. Just *how* the concept of requisites can *best* assist the study of the empirical world is, as we have just seen, a matter over which there is a diversity of opinion.

We have now completed our review of what makes functionalism unique as a theoretical perspective and methodological approach. Whether as a theory or a method, functionalism has been the subject of intense criticism. This criticism has often been more hysterical than insightful; and yet, there are a series of enduring problems which call into question the utility of this approach. We are now in a position to assess the merits of these criticisms in the next chapter. And depending upon the degree to which these criticisms are accepted, we can speculate in subsequent chapters on the future of this distinctive perspective.

5

The Emerging Critique

As a method and theoretical orientation, functionalism has been the subject of severe criticism. While a few early commentaries on the deficiencies of functionalism can be found,[1] the intense, and often vitriolic, critiques emerged in the 1950s and 1960s. In the end the questions raised by these criticisms have caused a sharp drop in the use of functional methods and theoretical concepts in both sociology and anthropology. However, before assessing whether or not the problems with functionalism are sufficient to warrant an obituary for this once dominant orientation, we should review the criticisms and examine their merits.

In this chapter, we will explore two lines of criticism: (1) those directed at the substantive image of the world connoted by the functional orientation, and (2) those concerning the logical traps inhering in the functional approach. To the degree that functionalism cannot resolve either these substantive or logical problems, then its future as an approach for building theory or collecting data is seriously in doubt. But we should reserve final judgement until after we have determined the merits of the criticisms.

[1] Leslie A. White, "History, Evolutionism and Functionalism: Three Types of Interpretation of Culture," *Southwestern Journal of Anthropology,* 1 (Summer, 1945):221–248; M. Spiro, "A Typology of Functional Analysis," *Explorations,* 1 (1953); S. F. Nadel, *Foundations of Social Anthropology* (Glencoe, Ill.: Free Press, 1951), p. 375. A more recent, interdisciplinary set of critiques can be found in Don Martindale, ed., *Functionalism in the Social Sciences* (Philadelphia: American Academy of Political and Social Science, 1965).

Substantive Problems with Functionalism

When we address "substantive" problems, we are concerned with the image of social reality connoted by a perspective. Does a theoretical perspective or methodological approach distort reality?[2] Are so many fundamental social processes and structures ignored by a perspective that its utility is questionable? These are substantive questions, and far more than any theoretical perspective in the social sciences, they have been consistently raised with regard to functionalism.

We will focus on three lines of substantive criticism: (1) the view that functionalism does not, and cannot, portray the historical events leading to the present profile of a social system; (2) the charge that functionalism reveals a conservative bias which is supportive of the status quo in a system; and (3) the related contention that functionalism cannot adequately account for social change. Each of these changes is examined below.

IS FUNCTIONALISM AHISTORICAL?

As we saw in Chapter 1, Durkheim's functional approach was decidedly historical in that he sought to understand the past causes of present events and to separate such causes from their functions. Yet, Durkheim's analysis of "history" was always analytical in that he attempted to portray how general classes of events cause other general types of events. Thus, for example, he was not concerned with the division of labor in a specific social system,[3] but with the forces in all systems that would result in its differentiation. Or, to take another example, Durkheim was not primarily interested in the specific causes of totemic worship among the Arunta, but more fundamentally he was preoccupied with what general conditions in human affairs would cause religious behavior in all social systems.[4]

---

[2]Naturally, all concepts distort, to some degree, the reality that they denote. The question is: How much distortion occurs? If vital processes are ignored, then the distortion can be seen as too great.

[3]Émile Durkheim, *The Division of Labor in Society* (New York: Free Press, 1933). Of course, Durkheim had a moral commitment to the unification of France, and he sought to legitimate his moral commitments with analytical statements. Such a strategy was consistent with Comte's view of a "science of society" allowing for the creation of a "good society." *See* Chapter 1.

[4]Émile Durkheim, *The Elementary Forms of the Religious Life* (New York: Free Press, 1948). Durkheim was also interested in discovering how moral integration operates in order that he could guide the moral re-integration of France.

Early functionalism, then, was not historiography; it was not involved in recording actual historical events in specific empirical systems. Such an exercise, Durkheim would have argued, is descriptive and *a*theoretical. However, to the degree that functionalists wish to understand a particular social system, they must direct attention to the concrete historical facts which caused the emergence of particular structures and processes of interest to an investigator of that system.

This kind of detailed tracing of historical events was, as we saw in Chapter 2, to be discouraged as anthropologists adopted Durkheim's functionalism to fit their purposes. As we emphasized, Malinowski and Radcliffe-Brown were reacting against naive evolutionalism and radical historical reconstruction.[5] Moreover, among traditional peoples, an examination of history is frequently impossible since written records of the past do not exist and since verbal accounts are, at best, fragmentary and idealized. For anthropologists, then, functionalism provided an alternative to historical or diacronic accounts, since it allowed them to examine social systems synchronically—that is, as a dynamic whole of interdependent parts operating to maintain that whole at a single point in time.

Explanations of why a part should exist in a contemporary system involved the use of a "social selection" mechanism: a part exists, in all probability, because it meets a system requisite or a need of individuals and hence had, and now has, selective advantage over other parts for the survival of individuals and the systemic whole.[6] Such an explanation presents, as we will examine shortly, a number of logical problems, but substantively it is clearly used to bypass the question of history.

More modern anthropological functionalism, such as Piddocke's[7] analysis of the Potlatch, combines a concern with historical events and the invocation of a social selection mechanism: the Potlatch represented a solution to historical problems encountered by the Kwakiutl in sustaining

---

[5]*See* Chapter 2 for details of the argument and relevant references.

[6]*See,* in particular, Figures 4.2, 4.3, and 4.4 of Chapter 4.

[7]Stuart Piddocke, "The Potlatch System of the Southern Kwakiutl: A New Perspective" in A. P. Vayda, ed., *Environment and Cultural Behavior* (Garden City, N.Y.: Natural History Press, 1969).

certain subpopulations. Yet, as Orans[8] and others note, the historical account offered by Piddocke is questionable and appears subordinate to the use of the social selection argument, resulting in a situation where functional analysis bends history to suit its purposes. In Piddocke's case, this involves the assertion that the Potlatch meets certain needs and hence had, and now has, a selective advantage over alternative practices—an assertion that, despite its historical trimmings, is similar to that of Malinowski and Radcliffe-Brown.

Anthropological functionalism, such as Goldschmidt's comparative functions approach or even Malinowski's comparative institutions strategy,[9] is also ahistorical. The strategy here is to gather comparable data on diverse systems in order to build theory. Concern is not on why and how a structure came to exist, but on understanding how it currently operates or functions in a system and is similar (or dissimilar) to parts in other systems.

Modern sociological functionalism also tends to be ahistorical. Parsons' early mechanism-equilibrium analysis concentrates on events in the present as they operate to maintain the system.[10] Merton's "net balance of functions" approach does not preclude historical accounts, but it directs an investigator's attention to assessing the functional consequences of a given part or process on specific system referents.[11] Parsons' later requisite functionalism similarly channels attention to the present consequences of parts for meeting one of four requisites and to the interchanges among parts having these diverse functions. Parsons' most recent concern with social evolution among Western societies does, however, reveal a concern with historical events, demonstrating that, given the inclination, a functional approach can be used to interpret the historical record.[12]

[8]Martin Orans, "Domesticating the Functional Dragon: An Analysis of Piddocke's Potlatch," *American Anthropologist,* 77 (1975):312–327.

[9]*See* Chapters 2 and 3 for details of their comparative methodologies.

[10]*See* Chapter 3 for details of sociological functionalism.

[11]We should note that Merton displays rare genius, especially among sociologists, in his historical analyses of specific topics. Yet, his formal functional paradigm does not sensitize investigators to historical antecedents.

[12]*See* his, "Evolutionary Universals," *American Sociological Review,* 29 (June, 1964):339–57; *Societies: Evolutionary and Comparative Perspectives* (Englewood Cliffs, N.J.: Prentice-Hall, 1966); and *The System of Modern Societies* (Englewood Cliffs, N.J.: Prentice-Hall, 1971).

In general, we can conclude that functionalism was preserved largely because it provided an ahistorical way to
examine traditional social systems. This bias has been retained among sociologists, although recent work has tended
to be more historical. We can now ask: Is there something
inherent in functionalism that discourages historical inquiry? Or, has the lack of historical inquiry simply been a
result of the personal preferences of various practitioners?
We might begin to answer these questions by stating at the
outset that functionalism does not deviate from most social
science inquiry, since social scientists, in general, tend toward ahistoricism.[13] And, in fact, among the few instances
of historical social science inquiry, the most penetrating
have been performed by those scholars who are considered
functionalists.[14]

More fundamentally, we need to ask the question: Should
social scientists be engaged in historical analyses? It is all
too easy to answer in the affirmative, but we might do well
to look at this question more carefully. To the degree that a
sociologist or social anthropologist wants to know why a
given part of a particular system exists, then an historical
analysis, if possible, of its causes is essential. Since much
functional analysis does consist of trying to understand why
a part exists, it should direct attention to historical causes
as well as functions. As we have seen, the social selection
mechanism is frequently invoked when the historical
record is cloudy or when the analyst is not inclined toward
historical inquiry. Hence, functionalism clearly has been
used as a way of avoiding historical analysis of empirical
systems.

Yet, to the degree that the analyst's concern is with generating abstract laws or principles of human organization,
rather than causal descriptions of why particular parts in
concrete systems should exist, then historical records are
inherently no better than other data sources. They are prob-

---

[13]There are, of course, a number of notable exceptions.

[14]For example, Robert K. Merton, Talcott Parsons, Kingsley Davis, and Marion
J. Levy, and Wilbert E. Moore have all, in a wide variety of contexts, performed
important historical analyses—probably among the very best in the social
sciences.

ably a bit worse since they are likely to be incomplete and to reflect biases of those who compile the historical records of a society. Thus, if the social sciences seek to generate abstract theoretical principles, a concern with history is not absolutely essential, although no source of data on humans should be ignored. And of course, this was the explicit point of Radcliffe-Brown's and Malinowski's, and probably Goldschmidt's implicit emphasis.

In sum, then, functionalism as used by its modern practitioners was not created to be historical; it was designed to facilitate the discovery of abstract laws and principles of human organization.[15] Yet, there is a contradiction in this emphasis: Radcliffe-Brown and Malinowski, as well as many anthropologists and sociologists alike, have often used functionalism to interpret and explain specific aspects of *concrete* systems. Such empirical investigation, where possible, probably *should be* historical, since specific phenomena have concrete causes in prior (historical) events. Thus, we can say that functionalism is inherently no more biased against history than other perspectives that seek to generate abstract laws; but since functionalism is also used as an empirical tool, its ahistorical emphasis is a clear liability to sound empirical inquiry.

Is FUNCTIONALISM CONSERVATIVE?
Beginning with Durkheim's concern with the integrative functions of the division of labor and religion, there can be little doubt that functionalism has been concerned with the consequences of system parts for maintaining social wholes. Radcliffe-Brown's functionalism always addressed the issue of the integrative consequences of a social structure, such as kinship. Malinowski's functionalism assessed the consequences of structures for meeting "needs" and "requisites." Parsons' early functionalism analyzes structures as instances of general mechanisms maintaining the "equilibrium," "homeostasis," or "moving equilibrium" of the social system. His later analysis focuses on the consequences of structures for meeting one of four universal functional requisites. Even Merton's strategy, which ex-

[15]We are not making judgments, at this point, as to whether or not functionalism actually does help the discovery of abstract laws.

plicitly introduces the notion of dysfunctions, typically concentrates on the positive functions of a structure and on how the "net balance of functions" is positive.

This apparent concern with order, stasis, equilibrium, integration, and the meeting of needs led in the 1950s to a series of criticisms of functionalism as conservative and as implicitly legitimizing the status quo.[16] Where, the critics asked, is a parallel concern with disorder, conflict, malintegration, oppression, dissensus, and disequilibrium? While defenders of functionalism could point to Durkheim's analysis of anomie, Parsons' insights on deviance and revolution, and Merton's discussion of bureaucratic dysfunctions and rebellion, there is some merit to the critics' charge. Functionalists seem to be fascinated with what holds society together—a question that is indeed at the crux of understanding human organization.

It is one matter to decry the lack of concern with disorder on the part of particular practitioners of functionalism, but it is a much more important matter to assert that functionalism is inherently conservative. We should be most concerned with this latter issue. All functionalists share a concern with assessing the consequences of a system part for other parts and systemic wholes, and at times, for needs and requisites imputed to parts and wholes. There is nothing substantively or logically conservative in this emphasis. A part can destroy another part; it can rip apart a social whole, and it can fail to meet needs. There is nothing, for example, in Parsons' mechanism-equilibrium analysis that precludes investigation of mechanisms that fail to hold an equilibrium, or that produce conflict, alienation, and disorder. Or, in Parsons' later discussion of requisites, there does not seem to be any analytical barrier to investigating those situations where requisites fail to be met. Indeed, it might be possible to develop a typology of consequences for the systemic whole based upon which need is not met. If adap-

---

[16]A representative sampling of these critiques would include the following: David Lockwood, "Some Remarks on 'The Social System,'" *British Journal of Sociology,* 7 (June, 1956):134–146; Ralf Dahrendorf, "Out of Utopia: Toward a Reorientation of Sociological Analysis," *American Journal of Sociology,* 74 (September, 1958):115–127; Irving Louis Horowitz, "Consensus, Conflict, and Cooperation: A Sociological Inventory," *Social Forces,* 41 (December, 1962):177–188; Alvin W. Gouldner, *The Coming Crisis in Western Sociology* (New York: Basic Books, 1976).

tive problems are not resolved, then one set of disorders could be expected; if goal attainment problems are not met then another type of problem would be likely; and so on. In Merton's approach there is little to preclude the possibility that the "net balance of functions" is "negative," and depending on how negative, different types of social disorder could be anticipated.

In regard to the criticism that functionalism is political ideology which supports the status quo, we can point out that by concentrating on patterns of interdependence and on mechanisms maintaining a system, functionalists can make very radical statements.[17] For example, by showing the power of forces for social control and the interdependent nature of social reality, a functionalist is forced to conclude that *if* social change is desired then it will have to be radical and far-reaching, since it will go against entrenched powers and disrupt extended networks of interdependencies. Thus, there is nothing inherently conservative, in a political or ideological sense, about functional analysis. To the degree that some functional approaches are considered conservative, this is the result of either the practitioner's or critic's predilection to be conservative or to find conservatism.

In sum, then, functionalism is not necessarily conservative. Admittedly, there is little doubt that functional discussions, whether empirical or analytical, have tended to focus on social order.[18] But this tendency, we feel, is the result of the practitioners' fascination with how patterns of social organization are created and maintained. Functionalists who find disorder fascinating will not be inhibited by their functionalism.

Is Functionalism Unable to Analyze Change?

The issue of change is related to instability since those social systems that reveal disorder are subject to change. The

[17]For example, while not explicitly a functional work, the senior author's works: *American Society: Problems of Structure* (New York: Harper and Row, 1972) and *Social Problems in America* (New York: Harper and Row, 1977) are clearly radical, and at the same time, heavily influenced by functional thinking.

[18]There are, however, some notable exceptions. *See* Parsons' discussion of revolution in his *The Social System* (New York: Free Press, 1951); Robin M. Williams, Jr.'s analysis of intergroup tensions, "Conflict and Social Order: A Research Strategy for Complex Propositions," *Journal of Social Issues,* 28 (February, 1972):11–26. Consult the bibliography of this work for further references.

critics thus charge that because functionalism is conservative and evidences a static bias, it cannot, and does not, take account of social change, especially radical change.[19] We must therefore ask: Is there something about functionalism which prevents this perspective from examining social change, particularly radical alterations of social structure?

When we examine functionalists' work on this matter, it is clear that they frequently do not address the issue of change, and when change is analyzed, attention is on evolutionary rather than revolutionary forces. Comte, Spencer, and Durkheim, for example, were most concerned with the broad evolutionary process from simple to complex social systems. In a similar vein, Parsons, in his recent work on change,[20] deals with the broad patterns of evolutionary change, although critics conveniently ignore his discussion of revolution and change in his *The Social System.* While Merton[21] explores the impact of forces behind the scientific "revolution," he is clearly more interested in the overall movement of social systems from sacred to secular and from simple to complex. In contrast, Malinowski, Radcliffe-Brown and those who followed their lead rejected such evolutionism, focusing instead on patterns of integration, in particular cultural systems at only one point in time.[22]

Much of the emphasis among functionalists on stasis or on evolution stems from their individual intent and focus rather than from inherent weaknesses in functionalism, per se. Functionalists of Spencer's, Durkheim's, and Parsons' persuasion have preferred to examine macro changes over long periods of time. When a scholar "stands back" and takes the broad view, the sudden upheavals and turmoils of specific systems become less central to analysis.[23] Conversely, when examining change in a concrete system over the short run, conflict and revolution are more likely to become central variables, as Parsons makes clear in *The Social System.* It is anthropologists rather than sociologists who have tended to employ the functional approach in studying specific empirical systems, but the nature of the

[19]*See* Dahrendorf, op. cit.
[20]*See* note 12.
[21]*See* his *Social Theory and Social Structure* (New York: Free Press, 1968).
[22]*See* Chapter 4.
[23]Marxist sociologists would, of course, disagree with this statement.

societies that they typically study—traditional peoples—are not typified by revolutionary social change.[24]

We can now put our guiding question in perspective: Is there something about functionalism that precludes the examination of radical change or is the bias the result of intellectual focus and subject matter? We think that the latter is the case. It would seem that topics of interest to functionalists, such as the failure of socialization and social control mechanisms and a system's inability to meet individual and system requisites, can provide insight into sudden change in social systems.[25] The major failing of functionalists is their unwillingness to specify the types of failures in mechanisms or in meeting requisites that will produce various types of social change. What is needed, therefore, is a specification of what types of malintegration, anomie, breakdowns in mechanisms, or failures to meet needs will cause, under what conditions, what types of change in varying types of social systems. In fairness, however, we should emphasize that even "conflict sociology" has been deficient on this score.[26] But for our present purposes, we can conclude that there is nothing inherent in functionalism as an approach that precludes the analysis of change. Indeed, as a procedure that focuses on the consequences of parts for social wholes, it is well suited to the investigation of change in these social wholes.

In reviewing the three substantive criticisms of functionalism, then we can see that they have less merit than the critics contend. What investigators prefer to study is not the same matter as what a theoretical approach forces them to study. Far more serious, we feel, are the logical problems

[24]There are exceptions. *See,* for example: Edmund Leach, *The Political Systems of Highland Burma* (Boston: Beacon, 1954), and C. R. Hallpike, "Functionalist Interpretations of Primitive Warfare," *Man,* 8 (1973):451–470; and Andrew P. Vadya, "Expansion and Warfare Among Swidden Agriculturalists" in his *Environment and Cultural Behavior* (Garden City, N.Y.: Natural History Press, 1969), 202–220.

[25]In fact, as we emphasized in Chapter 3, Talcott Parsons' discussion of the cybernetic hierarchy of control explicitly seeks to deal with change producing interchanges among action systems. But for a logical analysis of problems in analyzing change in functionalism, *see:* Francesca Cancian, "Functional Analysis and Change," *American Sociological Review,* 25 (December, 1960):818–827.

[26]Jonathan H. Turner, "From Utopia to Where: A Critique of Ralf Dahrendorf's Conflict Theory," *Social Forces,* 52 (December, 1973):236–244; and "The Future of Conflict Theory" in Jonathan H. Turner, *The Structure of Sociological Theory,* revised edition, (Homewood, Ill.: The Dorsey Press, 1978).

encountered when using functionalism. And hence, before we appear to vindicate functionalism, we should explore these logical problems.

Logical Problems with Functionalism

Some of the first criticisms of functionalism came from philosophers who questioned the logic of the approach.[27] Generally, these criticisms revolve around two related issues: (1) the problem of illegitimate teleology, and (2) the problem of tautology. To the degree that functional explanations of the social world are illegitimate teleologies or tautologies, their utility in building sociological theory can be seriously questioned. Thus, we need to explore these two problems before assessing the future of functionalism.

THE PROBLEM OF ILLEGITIMATE TELEOLOGY

What is an Illegitimate Teleology?   When social processes and structures are organized to realize future ends or goals, they are teleological. Teleology is thus a concept denoting that purpose inheres in the social world; social events are often designed to meet specific goals, ends, and purposes: Individuals organize their present behaviors in pursuit of a future goal; organizations and groups typically reveal goals toward which their members' activities are coordinated; and even total societies usually have political subsystems which set society-wide goals and mobilize resources for their attainment. Thus, social theories that do not take into account the teleological nature of human action and organization are likely to be sadly deficient.

Yet, it is possible to construct *illegitimate* teleologies—to imply that purpose or end states guide human affairs when such is not the case.[28] An illegitimate teleology exists when

[27]For examples of these, *see:* Carl G. Hempel, "The Logic of Functional Analysis," in L. Gross, ed., *Symposium on Sociological Theory* (New York: Harper and Row, 1959); Ernest Nagel, "A Formalization of Functionalism" in his *Logic Without Metaphysics* (Glencoe, Ill.: The Free Press, 1966).

[28]For basic references on this issue, *see:* Jonathan H. Turner, *The Structure . . .,* op. cit., pp. 104–110; G. Bergman, "Purpose, Function and Scientific Explanation," *Acta Sociologica,* 5 (1962):225–228; J. Canfield, "Teleological Explanation in Biology," *The British Journal for the Philosophy of Science,* 14 (1964):285–295; K. Deutsch, "Mechanism, Teleology and Mind," *Philosophy and Phenomenological Research,* 12 (1951):185–223; C. J. Ducasse, "Explanation, Mechanism, and

it is presumed that social processes and structures come into existence and operate to meet end states or goals, *without* being able to document the causal sequences whereby end states create and regulate these structures and processes involved in their attainment. As Durkheim[29] warned, "social phenomena do not generally exist for the useful results they produce." The emergence of the division of labor, for example, may have been caused by forces that have nothing to do with the functions that the division of labor now serves. To assume that the need for integration —a purpose or end state—causes the division of labor is, in all likelihood, an illegitimate teleology since it is not possible to document the causal sequences whereby the need for integration initiates the division of labor.

As we noted in Chapter 1, Durkheim separated "causal" from "functional" analysis specifically to avoid the problems of illegitimate teleology. Yet, despite Durkheim's awareness of the dangers of viewing functions as the cause of events, his analysis implied that integrative needs cause the emergence of structures—whether it be the division of labor or religious rituals—that meet these needs. To the degree that Durkheim's analyses of social phenomena contain this implication, then it lapses into illegitimate teleological reasoning, since Durkheim did not document how, and through what specific causal processes, integrative needs cause those phenomena that meet these needs. Our guiding question thus becomes: Do other functionalisms also fall into this trap? Is there something about functionalism that encourages illegitimate teleological reasoning?

Teleological Implications of Functional Reasoning   As is clear from the summary of functional methods and models

---

Teleology," in H. Feigl and W. Sellars, eds., *Readings in Philosophical Analysis* (New York: Appleton, 1949); D. Emmet, *Function, Purpose and Powers* (London: Routledge-Kegan, 1958); L. S. Fever, "Causality in the Social Sciences," *Journal of Philosophy,* 51 (1, 1954):191–208; W. W. Isajiw, *Causation and Functionalism in Sociology* (New York: Schocken, 1968); A. Kaplan, "Non-causal Explanation," in D. Lerner, *Cause and Effect* (New York: Free Press, 1965); C. A. Mace, "Mechanical and Teleological Causation," Feigl and Sellars, I. Scheffler, "Thoughts on Teleology," *The British Journal for the Philosophy of Science,* 9 (6, 1958):265–284; P. Sztompka, "Teleological Language in Sociology," *The Polish Sociological Bulletin,* 3 (2, 1969):56–69 and *System and Function: Toward a Theory of Society* (New York: Academic Press, 1974).

[29] *The Rules of the Sociological Method* (New York: Free Press, 1938), p. 96.

in the last chapter, functionalism addresses the question of what consequences a system part has for other parts, and more typically, for the systemic whole. Is there a temptation in such an emphasis to view these consequences as causing the events that produce them? While Durkheim reluctantly and inadvertently fell into illegitimate teleological reasoning, Radcliffe-Brown appears to have plunged headlong into this intellectual morass by eliminating from functional analysis the search for historical causes. Rather, for Radcliffe-Brown a "sociological explanation" of the "origins" of a system part consisted of showing the "necessary conditions of existence" that the part meets.[30] Such "explanations" can easily be interpreted to mean that the necessary condition causes the emergence and persistence of a system part. Malinowski similarly tended to view institutions as arising in response to basic and derived needs that they resolve. Parsons' mechanism-equilibrium analysis is explicitly teleological, since mechanisms are activated to reestablish the equilibrium.[31] Yet, without specifying precisely how these mechanisms are activated and how they operate to produce a preconceived state of normality or equilibrium, Parsons' early scheme runs the risk of being an illegitimate teleology. His later requisite orientation[32] can also imply that the functional requisites bring about the existence and persistence of the structures that meet these requisites. Merton's[33] net balance of functions approach is probably less susceptible to illegitimate teleologies, although several of his empirical illustrations often imply that the functions served by a part cause this part to emerge.[34] However, Goldschmidt's[35] comparative approach and other methodological strategies tend to avoid the problem of illegitimate teleology, since there is no effort to explain why a part exists and persists. Instead, attention is on the comparison of system parts and their consequences for

[30]*See,* in particular, his *Structure and Function in Primitive Society* (London: Cohen and West, 1952), p. 3.

[31]Talcott Parsons, *The Social System,* op. cit.

[32]*See* Chapter 3.

[33]Robert K. Merton, "Manifest and Latent Functions," *Social Theory and Social Structure,* op. cit.

[34]*See,* for example, Turner, *The Structure . . . ,* op. cit., pp. 69–91.

[35]Walter L. Goldschmidt, *Comparative Functionalism* (Berkeley: University of California Press, 1966).

resolving certain system problems. But most functional explanations in anthropology, such as Piddocke's[36] explanation of the Potlatch, imply that a need causes the events that meet this need.

Obviously, all functional theorists are aware of the problem and take steps to avoid constructing illegitimate teleologies. The most typical tact has been to invoke a "social selection" mechanism. Social structures are thus viewed as emerging because they have advantage over alternative structures in facilitating system adaptation to its environment, and hence, they have "survived." Such reference to how social selection produces a system part allows anthropologists to avoid discussing historical causes in the face of little data on a society's history. Moreover, invocation of the social selection mechanism has been applied not only to the historical emergence of social patterns, but also to their persistence: a social structure presently persists because it continues to facilitate the survival of the systemic whole.

There is probably some justification for the emphasis on social selection among those studying traditional societies. Anthropological ethnographers probably feel that they can see, in a very direct and real sense, how a structure has selective advantages over alternatives in a particular environment. Indeed, anthropologists typically study cultural systems in which insulation from the environment is not great and in which survival is problematic. For example, to not have a kinship system in a horticultural society that provides a basis for distribution of land tenure would decrease the survival capacity of the system. However, among sociologists who more typically study modern societies, it is often difficult to view the elaborated and differentiated social structures of an industrial, urban social system as the result of "social selection" in the face of impending and immediate threats of nonsurvival. Tradition, conquest, power, the preservation of privilege, innovation, institutional accommodation, and many other forces that have little to do with "survival" are more often viewed as the causes of particular structural patterns. And despite the immediacy with which the environment impinges upon

---

[36]Piddocke, op. cit.

traditional peoples, we think that the same is probably true of those traditional societies studied by anthropologists, and thus we should question the utility of "social selection" as a very precise way of understanding why a structure should exist and persist in a given system. This is not to deny that social selection does at times operate, but we should look more carefully at explanations that rely on this process.

"Social Selection" and Teleology   In many ways the use of a social selection mechanism becomes a gloss for an illegitimate teleology. To test the explanation that a structure exists because it has selective advantage requires several types of information. We would need information on a comparable system which did not survive because it lacked the structure under investigation. Anthropologists and sociologists would be hard pressed to find comparable systems alike in every respect except for one structure. To avoid this problem, we might reformulate our notion of "social selection": A structure exists because it has selective advantage in meeting a clearly defined functional need or requisite. Here, we need not posit the "life or death" of a system, but only state that social systems will reveal considerable turmoil and conflict if they cannot meet all their requisites, whether these be "universal" or "empirically established." The problem with this explanation is that we need clear criteria for determining when a requisite is not being met. How much, or little, integration constitutes "meeting this requisite"? When do we say that a system is not meeting its "adaptive needs"? And so on? Sociologists and anthropologists, unlike physicians, are not in a very good position to know what social "health" and "pathology" are.[37] And since we do not know, in terms of objective criteria, what a "normal" society is, we cannot easily determine if the requisites or needs of the "normal society" are being met. This same argument applies to notions of "equilibrium" or "homeostasis"; how do social scientists establish the ideal "normal state" for which certain social structures presumably have a selective advantage in maintaining?

Thus, the social selection explanation often becomes a

[37]Physicians do not know what ultimate "health" is, but they have operational indicators of both health and pathology. Social scientists do not have such objective indicators of social "health" and "pathology."

way of asserting that needs, requisites, normalcy, equilibrium, and other end states produce and maintain those structures which meet needs, promote survival, achieve equilibrium, and restore normalcy. No causal statements as to how, and through what processes, such end states set up selective pressures for the emergence and persistence of structures are typically offered. And given the virtual impossibility of finding instances of matched surviving and nonsurviving systems and establishing cut-off points for survival or for what constitutes not meeting a requisite, the social selection argument becomes a pseudo-explanation, disguising a hidden illegitimate teleology: the end state causes, in ways that are unspecified, those structures and processes that bring about this end state.

Not all social selection arguments are pseudo-explanations, however. Arthur Stinchcombe,[38] for example, has argued persuasively that some social processes operate as a "reverse causal chain." A certain trend—say, population growth or increases in organizational expansion—can occur until it can no longer continue. A profit making corporation, for instance, grows to a point until its profits decrease, and then, diversifies and divests. A population grows until Malthus' "four horsemen" curb its growth. There is no purpose implied in these explanations, and clear criteria as to when selection against a trend occurs can be established—for the case of organizational growth, a decrease in profits. Much social life is subject to such reverse causal chains, but functional analysis does not alert us to these processes any more than other theoretical perspectives. And moreover, these are limiting cases; many phenomena cannot be understood in terms of reverse causal chains. Thus, the operation of reverse causal chains in the social (as well as biological and physical) worlds does not obviate the problem of illegitimate teleology in functionalism.

Are Functional Explanations Illegitimate Teleologies?

What, then, can we conclude about the problem of illegitimate teleology in functional theory? Much of the problem,

---

[38]Arthur L. Stinchcombe, *Constructing Social Theories* (New York: Harcourt, Brace and World, 1968), p. 100.

we suspect, derives from the implicit organicism in functional theorizing. In an organism, "life" and "death" can be assessed and "pathological states" can be operationalized.[39] But what constitutes life, death, and pathology for societies is rather difficult to determine and hence the assessment of what a structure does for survival (or requisites) and/or for normalcy (or equilibrium and homeostasis) is not a simple task. Without this capacity to determine survival and non-survival or normalcy and pathology, explanations can become illegitimate teleologies. This is especially likely when historical analysis is not possible or eschewed. The result is for the existence and persistence of parts to be "explained" in terms of the needs or end states that they meet, without the necessary causal documentation. Thus, we can conclude that functional explanations often become illegitimate teleologies—a fact which seriously hampers functionalism's utility for understanding patterns of human organization.

THE PROBLEM OF TAUTOLOGY

A tautology is circular reasoning in which variables are defined in terms of each other, thus making causes and effects obscure and difficult to assess. In much functional analysis there is a danger of tautologous statements.[40] In mechanism-equilibrium analysis, for example, we sometimes find a statement like the following: The existing system is in equilibrium; a structure is a part of this system; therefore, it can be viewed as a mechanism maintaining the equilibrium. In this statement, the implied cause of the part is its function to maintain the equilibrium, while the cause of the equilibrium is the existence of the part. Or, to illustrate further, we can find statements from functional requisite analysis that argue the following: Because a struc-

[39]See Chapter 1 on the emergence of functionalism.
[40]For basic reference on this issue, see: Turner, The Structure . . . , op. cit., Chapter 5; Ronald Philip Dore, "Function and Cause," American Sociological Review, 26 (December, 1961):843–853; Charles J. Erasmus, "Obviating the Functions of Functionalism," Social Forces, 45 (March, 1967):319–328; R. B. Braithwaite, Scientific Explanation (London: Cambridge University Press, 1953), Chapters 4 and 10; Bernard Barber, "Structural-Functional Analysis: Some Problems and Misunderstandings," American Sociological Review, 21 (April, 1956): 129–135; Alvin W. Gouldner, "Reciprocity and Autonomy in Functional Theory" in Gross, op. cit.; Harold Fallding, "Functional Analysis in Sociology," American Sociological Review, 28 (February, 1963):5–13.

ture is a part of a system, it must be involved in meeting the system's needs, while the structure exists because a system's needs are met and the system survives. In both of these statements, it is difficult to know what causes what and the explanations seem circular. The basic contour of functional tautologies is outlined in Figure 5.1.

Many of Radcliffe-Brown's explanations are tautologies: a structure such as a kinship system meets the integrative needs of the systemic whole, while the persistence of the systemic whole allows the kinship system to persist. Malinowski often lapsed into tautologous reasoning: the institution arises to meet basic biological needs, while the persistence of the institution is assured because other, derived needs are met. More modern functionalists have been alert to the dangers of tautology, and indeed one still does not have to look very far to find them.

The most typical way of avoiding tautologous statements is, as with the related problem of illegitimate teleology, to invoke the social selection argument: Structures have selective advantages for resolving survival problems and/or equilibrium needs, and because they continue to be essential to system survival and to equilibrium maintenance, they remain as integral parts of the system. As we emphasized for the issue of teleology, however, this argument is only viable when (a) instances of nonsurvival and disequi-

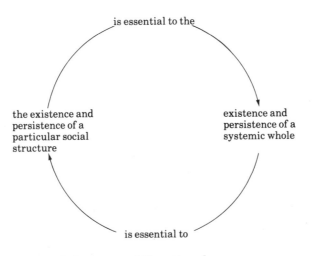

FIGURE 5.1   General Contours of Functional
Tautologies

librium in comparable systems without a particular part can be found; and (b) clear criteria as to what constitutes "survival" and "equilibrium" can be established. Rarely are sociologists and social anthropologists in a position to provide either of these essential pieces of information. The result is for many functional statements to be circular, as is emphasized in Figure 5.1.

Summary and Conclusion

We are now in a position to assess the criticisms of functionalism. These criticisms have been divided into substantive and logical. We now should review each of these and indicate ways in which they are related.

As we have stressed, functionalism is not well suited to the study of historical causes, but it appears no more deficient on this score than other theoretical perspectives. The tautological nature of many functional arguments perhaps underscores why it is that functional accounts are ahistorical. The use of the "social selection" metaphor to obviate the logical problems of illegitimate teleology and tautology only heightens the inability of this orientation, as presently used by social scientists, to provide insights into historical causes.

The related charges that functionalism (a) evidences a static bias, (b) reveals an inability to deal with radical change, and (c) supports the status quo have less merit than is commonly believed. Again, much of the apparent conservatism of the perspective stems from efforts to avoid logical problems by viewing structures as having selective advantages for maintaining social systems. By trying to explain why a structure exists and persists, functionalists have connoted an image of social organization as integrated, orderly,. and unchanging. But, as we have emphasized, there is nothing compelling in the logic of functionalism that requires this emphasis. Structures can fail to have selective advantage; they can reduce the effectiveness of other structures; and they can create internal and external strains that result in change of social systems.

More serious than these substantive problems, we feel, are the logical hazards confronted when performing functional analysis. Illegitimate teleologies and tautologous statements abound in functional explanations, primarily because the causal relations between parts and systemic wholes are not adequately specified. The emphasis on part-to-whole relations, and the corresponding de-emphasis on the historical causes of parts, often makes functional statements illegitimate teleologies and tautologies, or both.

In sum, then, the substantive problems of functional analysis can be overcome with minimal effort. The logical problems, we feel, pose such difficulties that a radical transformation in the functional orientation is required. The future of functionalism as a viable intellectual tool in the social sciences hinges on whether or not this transformation can occur. In the next chapter we explore the future of functionalism and offer some suggestions for how functionalism can be profitably used by social scientists.

6

The Future of Functionalism

The Appeal of Functionalism

Much of the appeal of functionalism resides in its efforts to address the question: What does a structure do for society? In borrowing from biology a concern with how parts maintain the "body social," Comte was able to draw attention to sociology and to legitimate the new "science of society." Spencer, in making the distinction between "structure" and "function," alerted the sociological consciousness to a concern with assessing how social structures operate to maintain and change the larger social context. Durkheim codified this line of reasoning into rules of the sociological method that were used to explore the integrative functions of such diverse structural patterns as the division of labor and religious ritual.

Radcliffe-Brown, as one of the key figures involved in the preservation of functionalism, adopted the Durkheimian tradition and began to assess structures in terms of how they resolve integrative problems. Malinowski expanded this type of analysis by suggesting that sociologists and social anthropologists could assess not only what a structure does for society but also for individual biological needs. Moreover, he began to catalogue different types of needs of different system referents, thus expanding the basic functional question to: What does a social structure "do for" individuals and society?

128

Modern functionalists have continued to ask this appealing question. Parsons has asked what system parts do for meeting the needs of an overall action system or for specific subsystems. Merton has argued for assessments of structures in terms of how well they meet empirically established needs of individuals and social systems. And Goldschmidt has stressed the utility of using notions of functional requisites as a way for ordering and comparing data on diverse social systems.

Basic to all these varying points of emphasis, then, are some key assumptions that make functional analysis appealing:[1]

1. The social world tends to be ordered into systems composed of interrelated parts.
2. If these systems are to persist and survive, certain problems confronting their constituent members, their subsystems, and their overall structure must be resolved.
3. "Understanding" of the social world is therefore facilitated when knowledge about how a structure operates, or fails to operate, to resolve these problems is secured.

Just what constitutes "understanding" of social phenomena, however, has been variously interpreted by those using the functional approach. Anthropologists such as Malinowski[2] and Goldschmidt[3] have emphasized that assessment of how structures resolve basic human and organizational problems can provide a basis for ordering data and thereby facilitate the process of "understanding" regularities in the data. From these regularities, explanatory theories can be induced, or conversely, existing theories can be tested against the facts ordered by a functional method. For sociologists such as Merton,[4] Parsons,[5] Davis,[6] Moore,[7] and Levy[8]

[1]Jonathan H. Turner, "The Future of Functionalism" in *The Structure of Sociological Theory,* revised edition (Homewood, Ill.: The Dorsey Press, 1978).

[2]Bronislaw Malinowski, *A Scientific Theory of Culture* (Chapel Hill: University of North Carolina Press, 1944).

[3]Walter L. Goldschmidt, *Comparative Functionalism* (Berkeley: University of California Press, 1966).

[4]Robert K. Merton, "Manifest and Latent Functions" in *Social Theory and Social Structure* (New York: Free Press, 1968). *See* Chapter 3.

[5]Talcott Parsons, "The Present Position and Prospects of Systematic Theory in Sociology" in *Essays in Sociological Theory* (New York: Free Press, 1949).

functionalism has, at different points in their work, been viewed as a way of generating "understanding" through theoretical explanation. Notions of requisites are not just methodological tools; they are also key concepts that will be incorporated into theoretical propositions, and ultimately, into the laws of human organization.

In this chapter on the future of functionalism, therefore, we need to determine if both of these notions of what constitutes "understanding" are intellectually viable. As we will argue, the future of functionalism as theoretical explanation is probably less viable than its future as a methodological tool that can facilitate research inquiry and theoretical induction. At the same time we should seek to portray a future for functionalism that retains what scholars and laypersons alike find most appealing about this perspective— that is, its attention to the question of what social structures and processes "do for" individuals and society. A science of society which does not ask this question runs the risk of ignoring one of the most intriguing questions that humans can ask about themselves and the social world around them. Yet, a science that fails to recognize the problems inhering in this question will not be a true science.

Avoiding the Problems of Functionalism

AN ALTERNATIVE PART-WHOLE CAUSAL ANALYSIS
As we have emphasized, functionalism originally emerged out of organismic doctrines which viewed society as a type of organism. The extremes of such organicism have been gradually mitigated to the point that functional analysis now concerns the relation of interrelated parts to various states of social wholes—these "states" usually being assessed in terms of "needs," "requisites," "survival," and "equilibrium." And, as we have also emphasized, this stress on what parts "do for" these states of the social whole presents many problems when functionalism is used as an *explanation* of parts and wholes. It would be unfortunate,

---

[6]Kingsley Davis, *Human Societies* (New York: Macmillan, 1949) and "Some Principles of Stratification," *American Sociological Review,* 10 (April, 1945):242–247.

[7]Ibid.

[8]Marion J. Levy, *The Structure of Society* (Princeton, N.J.: Princeton University Press, 1952).

however, if this concern with part-whole relations were rejected because of the difficulties in generating unproblematic functional explanations.

How, then, do we retain this concern with part-whole analysis? The first step is to recognize that it will be difficult, in most circumstances, to document how needs, requisites, survival, equilibrium, or homeostasis are caused by, or are the cause of, parts that operate in relation to these states. Thus, when seeking to *explain* the causal relation between parts and wholes, assumptions about needs, requisites, survival, equilibrium, and homeostasis should be abandoned. Societies are clearly not organisms, and hence, we should abandon concepts that carry this connotation. Once these concepts, and all their hidden connotations are dropped, we can proceed with a simple causal analysis: How do variations in a part affect variations in clearly defined social wholes? Such a question does *not* ask: How do parts meet needs and requisites, or promote homeostasis or equilibrium? Rather, it asks that variations in a dependent variable—the social whole—be accounted for by variations in parts. Conversely, we can at times explore the reciprocal question: How do variations in the social whole cause variations in particular parts? Thus, when strict attention is paid to causality, the thrust of functional analysis can be retained, but as soon as assumptions of needs and equilibrium are introduced into the analysis, the logical problems encountered by virtually every functional scheme since Durkheim will surface again.

It can be argued, of course, that this minor adjustment in approach strips functional analysis of its distinctiveness. Such is probably the case, since we are advocating the abandonment of efforts to explain variations in parts and social wholes of many key concepts: function, survival, requisites, need, equilibrium, and homeostasis. These, we feel, are not useful concepts for explanation in the social sciences. The future of functionalism, we contend, resides in the rejection of some of its distinctive concepts as useful theoretical explanations of social phenomena.

REJECTING FUNCTIONAL EXPLANATIONS

The logical problems of tautology and illegitimate teleology surface when the concepts of functional needs and requisites, and related notions of equilibrium, become a part of an explanation of why a structure exists and persists.[9] These problems are not always insurmountable, but we can ask: Should we not avoid them by ceasing to engage in those forms of functional analysis where they consistently surface?

An affirmative answer to this question means that functionalism as an explanatory tool should be abandoned, while a negative answer assures that many functional explanations will be illegitimate teleologies and tautologous. Faced with this choice, we think that the future of functionalism resides in the recognition of its limitations. One such limitation is the inability of functional theoretical explanations to avoid, with sufficient consistency, certain logical problems. Functionalism, therefore, should not be viewed as theoretical explanation. Rather, it will be more useful to the social sciences as a heuristic device and methodological tool that can assist theorists using less problematic theory building strategies.[10]

This conclusion goes against what Durkheim felt was an essential rule for sociological explanation, what Radcliffe-Brown argued was the key to developing sociological laws, what Parsons views as necessary for abstract systems of concepts and theory, and what Merton feels is desirable for constructing middle range theories. It is more consistent with Goldschmidt's and Malinowski's emphasis, although we suspect that these two scholars have harbored, perhaps only implicitly, visions of functionalism as an explanatory tool. This vision should be extinguished, but such a conclusion should not be considered a rejection of functionalism as a method. Indeed, functionalism as a method for collecting and organizing data has much to offer a social science which has too easily become mired in descriptive accounts of empirical events.

USING FUNCTIONALISM AS A METHOD OF INQUIRY

In sociology, functionalism is usually regarded as the antithesis of empirical inquiry. Parsons and others have often been portrayed as "armchair" theorists who fail to "opera-

[9]*See* Chapter 5 for an elaboration of why this is so.
[10]*See* Jonathan H. Turner, op. cit., for an explication of some of these strategies.

tionalize" their concepts and who thereby have little to offer empirical researchers. In contrast, anthropological functionalism has been used to interpret specific ethnographic facts and has been tied to empirical inquiry. What accounts for this difference?

First, as we have noted previously, functionalism emerged in anthropology as an alternative way of interpreting specific sets of ethnographic data. In sociology, however, functionalism arose in response to efforts at creating a general system of explanation in a theoretical vacuum. Second, anthropology has a much less well developed division of labor between theorists and researchers than sociology. Thus, as anthropological functionalists document, there is no necessary reason for the impression in sociological circles that functionalism and empirical inquiry are at odds. Indeed, the universally acknowledged insightfulness of Parsons' essays on empirical topics (as opposed to his formal analytical works) should alert us to the fact that functionalism provides a way of penetrating the empirical world.

Therefore we must now ask, how can we use functionalism as a tool for getting a handle on the empirical world and for ordering and displaying data? There are, we feel, two distinctive approaches: (1) the comparative method, advocated by Goldschmidt and Malinowski, which we will term "comparative requisite analysis," and (2) a method that we can, for lack of a better label, term "holistic requisite analysis." Each of these is discussed below.

Comparative Requisite Analysis   One task of social scientists is to present data from diverse social systems in ways that allow for their comparison. For example, Max Weber advocated an "ideal type" methodology in which certain crucial features of a particular class of phenomena are accentuated and presented as a "pure" or "idealized" type which can then be used as an analytical yardstick for comparing different concrete empirical systems.[11] Thus, his famous ideal type of bureaucracy[12] was designed as a way of providing a standard frame of reference for comparing ac-

[11]Max Weber, *From Max Weber,* edited by H. Gerth and C. W. Mills (New York: Oxford, 1946), pp. 196–266.
[12]Ibid.

tual bureaucratic organizations in different social contexts. By recording each empirical system's deviations from the ideal type, it is then possible to compare these systems.[13]

The essence of anthropological inquiry resides in comparing data from diverse cultures. Malinowski sought to use "institutional elements," such as personnel, charter, norms, functions, and the like, as common categories that would allow for the display of data from different systems. George Murdock[14] has pursued a related strategy by creating the Human Area Relations Files in which social systems are broken down into "cultural traits" and then placed into standard categories, thereby making them amenable to statistical comparisons.

Walter Goldschmidt's comparative functionalism offers yet another approach to ordering cross cultural data.[15] Since we have summarized his strategy in Chapter 3, we need only highlight certain problems that his strategy avoids. First, by concentrating on "functions," or certain real and universal problems confronting humans and all patterns of social organization, many of the difficulties in making facts fit preconceived categories, such as those developed by Murdock in his HARF or Malinowski in his "institutional elements," are reduced. Second, definitional problems of trying to have widely diverse social patterns "fit" a standard definition of an institution like family or religion are obviated.

By detailing certain universal problems confronted by humans in social systems, and then, by describing the diverse ways peoples of the world go about dealing with these problems, Goldschmidt provides common analytical referents for comparing diverse social systems. Such a strategy is methodologically similar to Weber's ideal type approach, but it has one advantage: It does not employ an "idealized" or analytically "pure" yardstick, but one which makes reference to the real problems encountered by humans as biological and psychological creatures who create patterns of social organization. Thus, while Goldschmidt does not execute his strategy, except by example, he offers a way for

---

[13]*See* Chapter 4.
[14]George P. Murdock, *Social Structure* (New York: Macmillan Co., 1949).
[15]Walter Goldschmidt, op. cit.

functionalism to provide a useful method for ordering data drawn from diverse social systems.

What this methodological approach requires is a longer catalogue of basic biological, psychological, and organizational problems than is provided by Goldschmidt. Moreover, while some problems will be universal to all humans and all social systems, some problems will be typical of only certain types of systems. Goldschmidt terms these "contingent functions," because they are problems that are contingent upon a particular level of social structural (and perhaps psychological) elaboration. Thus, more comprehensive lists of these contingent problems will need to be constructed.

Such lists provide a yardstick for comparative *description.* They are not explanations of why these events so described should exist; such inferences are too likely to carry analysis into the logical problems discussed in the last chapter. But there is, of course, a hidden assumption in such lists: These problems *must* be resolved if a system is to remain viable in its environment, and therefore, descriptions of structural patterns that cohere around a problem are probably more crucial than descriptions of structural patterns or social processes that are not central to the resolution of a problem. Thus, not only is a common yardstick provided for comparative description, but this yardstick also provides a basis—albeit an assumptive basis—for sorting out "important" from unimportant social processes. If subsequent and *non*functional explanations of these facts do not confirm these assumptions about the utility of using functional problems to sort out critical events and structures, then they can be discarded as useful points of comparison.

Such a methodological strategy retains much that is appealing and intriguing about functionalism: The view that structures operate to resolve problems faced by humans, and therefore, "do something for" social systems. Yet, none of the presumptuousness of functionalism as theoretical explanation of events is retained. Naturally, comparative functionalism is not the only comparative method, but it could prove useful. To reject functionalism as totally unviable because of its problems as an explanatory device would be to abandon what could be a useful methodological tool.

The Holistic Requisite Method   Many scholars have commented on Talcott Parsons' genius for describing the important features of concrete empirical phenomena,[16] such as the American school classroom, the doctor-patient relationship, the political process in Nazi Germany, the American kinship system, and many other specific empirical events of particular social systems. One of the commonly expressed sentiments is that Parsons abandons his formal analytical scheme when performing such descriptions. We believe such sentiments could not be further from the truth, for it is more likely the case that he employs his conceptual scheme to sort out important from unimportant social processes and structures. His descriptions are so penetrating, we feel, precisely because he employs his schemes to penetrate into the workings of empirical events.

This fact suggests that, as a method for describing social systems, Parsons' requisite functionalism can prove a valuable tool. As long as we do not aspire to use his conceptual categories as theoretical explanation, his approach can provide guidance for those involved in describing social systems.

In his first work, *The Structure of Social Action,*[17] Parsons advocated a theoretical strategy termed "analytical realism." In this strategy he committed himself to developing "systems of concepts" that "adequately grasp" the critical features of the social world. We suspect that this strategy represents an adoption and modification of Weber's ideal type methodology, since Parsons' "theory of action" looks more like a "categorization of action." Parsons has thus felt that developing a system of categories that accurately reflect properties of the world is logically a prior step to developing a system of propositions, principles, or laws. This strategy has come under considerable criticism,[18] but it

[16]A partial list of such descriptions would include: *Family, Socialization and Interaction Process* (New York: Free Press, 1955); "The School Class as a Social System," *Harvard Education Review,* 54 (Fall, 1959):487–99; "Youth in the Context of American Society," *Daedalus,* 28 (Winter, 1961); most of the articles in *Essays in Sociological Theory* (New York: Free Press, 1954); and sections on the "doctor-patient relationship" in *The Social System,* op. cit.

[17]Talcott Parsons, *The Structure of Social Action* (New York: McGraw-Hill, 1937).

[18]Austin T. Turk, "On the Parsonian Approach to Theory Construction," *Sociological Quarterly,* 8 (Winter, 1967):37–49.

should alert us to the classificatory nature of the Parsonian scheme. While this nature does not totally preclude the development of social laws, it is far more useful as a methodological device.

Parsons' scheme is particularly useful when trying to describe an entire social system. Without a priori categories for sorting through the maze of empirical events constantly occurring in any empirical system, efforts at descriptions will be thwarted. And in contrast to Goldschmidt's comparative functionalism, Parsons' system of categories makes claims to exhaustiveness in its capacity to capture all of the salient features of a social system. Thus, the scheme is best employed when efforts are undertaken to describe a coherent and complex social whole.

Parsons provides three types of criteria for sorting out important from less important social processes: (1) the four system requisites, (2) the analytical linkages among system sectors, and (3) the generalized media of exchange. Each of these is discussed below.

(1) In asserting that all action systems evidence four functional requisites[19]—that is, adaptation, goal attainment, integration, and latency—Parsons provides researchers with a standardized set of criteria for assessing the importance of social events. Those processes in a social whole that are directly involved in resolving adaptive, goal attainment, integration, and latency problems are the most important objectives of inquiry. Processes that are not directly pertinent to these problems are likely to be less critical in understanding the social whole. In fact, it might be asserted that the degree of involvement of structures and processes in any of these four requisites can dictate the degree to which empirical researchers should focus their efforts on these structures and processes.

For example, Parsons' scheme argues that, if investigators wish to grasp how a system operates, an important area of inquiry should involve an examination of those processes and structures involved in securing resources, converting them into usable commodities and facilities, and then distributing them to other system units. That is, researchers should investigate the problem of "adaptation" as faced by

---

[19]*See* page 25 for a definition of each.

any empirical system. At the societal level, this inquiry would focus on economic structures and processes, while in other social systems, such as a small group, a bureaucracy or a community, other non-economic resources might be important topics. Similar examination of social systems with respect to goal attainment, latency, and integration is also dictated by the Parsonian scheme.

The strength of Parsons' requisites is that they are the same for all types of social systems. Investigators thus have similar criteria for assessing the importance of structures and processes in all varieties of systems, from a small group to a system of societies. The fact that Parsons has provided some of the most insightful *descriptions* in the social science literature of a wide range of empirical systems[20]—from the school classroom and American family to the development of a system of modern societies[21]—should attest to the utility of employing his four functional requisites as a methodological device. Data collection and arrangement with reference to Parsons' criteria are likely, we feel, to be useful in creating and testing *non*functional theoretical propositions and principles.

(2) In Figure 3.3 of Chapter 3, we presented Parsons' and Smelser's vision of key points of interaction among functional sectors of societal systems (see page 77).[22] This table provides yet another type of methodological tool for empirical descriptions, since it establishes a set of criteria for assessing critical interactions among key structures. Thus, for example, an important point of interaction to observe is the exchange of "capital" for "productivity" (numbers (1) and (2) in Figure 3.3). While Parsons and Smelser developed this scheme for societal systems, there is little to preclude the investigation of other types of social systems with this methodological tool. For instance, it would be quite useful to describe how "task leaders" in a small group allocate "capital" to other group members in order to facilitate their "productivity." Indeed, Parsons has provided us with a somewhat novel way of viewing small group processes—a

[20]*See* note 16.

[21]*See* his *Societies: Evolutionary and Comparative Perspectives* (Englewood Cliffs, N.J.: Prentice Hall, 1966), and *The System of Modern Societies* (Englewood Cliffs, N.J.: Prentice Hall, 1971).

[22]Talcott Parsons and Neil J. Smelser, *Economy and Society* (New York: Free Press, 1956).

way, we feel, which may be far superior to the manner in which small group processes are often described.[23] We may not be accustomed to viewing leaders as providing "capital" or group members as engaging in "productivity," but once we accept this as an important point of interaction in a small group, then we can set about describing the nature of capital resources available and the ways that these are exchanged for productivity. Similar descriptions are possible for the other twelve points of interaction outlined in Figure 3.3. By carefully exploring these interactions, an extremely insightful description of a social system would result, whether this system be a small group or a system of societies.

Once again, the strength of Parsons' approach resides in the common reference point that his system of categories provides. By providing investigators with a standard set of exchanges to explore in different types of social wholes, descriptions will yield comparable information that can be used to create or test nonfunctional theories.

(3) Parsons' more recent concern with generalized media of exchange could potentially provide another set of methodological criteria for examining processes in social systems. By stressing that investigators concentrate on the use and exchange of distinctive media, Parsons asserts that, if social systems are to be adequately described, the nature of the symbolic media[24]—whether money, commitments, influence, or power—employed by different social units must be explored.

Since Parsons has yet to work out his ideas on symbolic media, however, we feel that the vagueness of conceptualization renders this aspect of his conceptual scheme less useful as a methodological tool. With refinement, though, it might be a constructive methodology for generating descriptions of an often ignored social process.

---

[23]Parsons and Robert F. Bales, a prominent small group researcher, worked together in developing many aspects of the Parsonian scheme. *See:* Talcott Parsons, Robert F. Bales, and Edward A. Shils, *Working Papers in the Theory of Action* (Glencoe, Ill.: Free Press, 1953).

[24]*See:* "On the Concept of Political Power," *Proceedings of the American Philosophical Society,* 107 (June, 1963):232–62; "On the Concept of Influence," *Public Opinion Quarterly,* 27 (Spring, 1963): 37–62; "Some Problems of General Theory" in J. C. McKinney and E. A. Tiryakian, eds. *Theoretical Sociology: Perspectives and Developments* (New York: Appleton-Century Crofts, 1970), pp. 28–68.

In sum, then, we have argued that key elements in Parsons' functional "theory" can provide investigators with common criteria for describing structures and processes in social systems. Much description work in sociology and anthropology is unstructured, unsystematic, and unusable as a data base for theory building and testing. Parsons' four requisites, analytical interchanges, and generalized media provide a way to "grasp" complex systemic wholes in terms of common categories. Moreover, these categories are not trivial, but are founded on an explicit assumption about what is most important for investigators to know. In disciplines that do not have well developed theories to guide research and which, for better or worse, seem to be committed to inductive methods,[25] Parsons' system of categories can perhaps be useful in making descriptions more structured, systematic, and usable for theory building. This conclusion is, of course, the exact opposite of that usually reserved for Parsonian functionalism. Parsons' scheme is portrayed as too abstract and too vague to be useful, but on the contrary, its abstractness allows investigators to see the common elements of social systems and to approach their study with a general, rather than highly specific and constraining, set of analytical criteria.

Summary and Conclusion

We have now come to an end in our review of functionalism in the social sciences, particularly in sociology and anthropology where it has, until recently, been the dominant orientation. We have stressed that functionalism asks a most appealing question: What do system parts "do for" individuals and society? A perspective that attempts to build theoretical explanations around this question is likely to fall prey to the logical problems of tautology and illegitimate teleology. But a perspective that seeks to provide criteria for generating descriptions of how social systems operate is likely to facilitate the collection and display of data sets that can be used to generate and test theories.

[25]We question whether general theories are ever inducted. The great theoretical breakthroughs in science have typically come from deductive efforts. Yet, intellectual work in sociology and anthropology is typically empirical. There are few purely deductive works in these disciplines.

Thus, functionalism as an explanatory theory is, we feel, "dead" and continued efforts to use functionalism as a theoretical explanation should be abandoned in favor of more promising theoretical perspectives. As a method, however, functionalism has much to offer a social science which is often overwhelmed by its existing data sets and chaotic in its collection of additional sets.

Contrary to many of the sociological critiques, then, functionalism can facilitate, not impede as the critiques so incorrectly presume, the collection and display of cross-cultural and intrasystemic data. This book can thus be considered to be a sympathetic and remorseful obituary to functionalism as theory, but it can also be seen to offer a modest proposal for the rebirth of functionalism as a useful method in the social sciences.

Index

Aberle, David, 60–61
Adler, Mortimer, 38
A, G, I, L scheme (Parsons), 75–80
Andaman Islanders, 35, 37, 42, 43, 86
Andaman Islanders, The (Radcliffe-Brown), 37
Arunta people, 23, 109
Australian aborginals, 23, 33

Benedict, Ruth, 32
Boas, Franz, 31–32
British tradition, 8, 14

Cohen, Albert, 60–61
Comte, Auguste, 12, 14, 20, 29, 70, 73, 83, 93, 96, 116, 128
  and the British tradition in science, 8–9
  concerned with social conditions in France, 2–3
  defines purpose of sociology, 4
  defines theory of organicism, 5–7
  develops doctrine of social progress, 3–5
  welds sociology to empirical inquiry, 4
Course of Positive Philosophy (Comte), 3

Darwin, Charles, 6, 8, 12
Davis, Kingsley, 46, 61, 62, 95, 129–30
  develops theory of stratification, 59–60
Davis-Moore Hypothesis, The, 59–60, 61, 67, 68
Diachronic analysis, 40
Diffusionism, doctrine of, 30–31, 35, 38, 46–47, 55
Division of Labor in Society, The, (Durkheim), 16–20, 36
Durkheim, Émile, and aboriginal tribes, 23–26
  and the anthropological tradition, 28–29
  and the appeal of his functional approach, 35–36, 93
  and the British tradition, 15

143